95-

GW00382777

ROYAL PARKS FOR THE PEOPLE

ROYAL PARKS FOR THE PEOPLE

London's Ten

HAZEL THURSTON

DAVID & CHARLES

NEWTON ABBOT   LONDON

NORTH POMFRET (VT)   VANCOUVER

For Carol 'David' Chambers, with love

0 7153 6454 5

Set in 11 on 13pt Centaur and printed in
Great Britain by Latimer Trend &
Company Ltd Plymouth for David &
Charles (Holdings) Limited South
Devon House Newton Abbot Devon

Published in the United States of
America by David & Charles Inc
North Pomfret Vermont 05053 USA

Published in Canada by Douglas David
& Charles Limited 3645 McKechnie
Drive West Vancouver BC

CONTENTS

LIST OF ILLUSTRATIONS

INTRODUCTION

London's Royal Parks are very special places, because the metropolis and its conurbation have spread around their almost sacrosanct boundaries instead of these being constrained to meet the importunate needs of rapid urban development. This has guaranteed the parks an integrity which is sometimes lacking in otherwise excellent drawing-board design. In almost every instance the feeling of space is superb, as might be expected in the work of English masters in the art of landscaping, whose designs were incorporated into the scene rather than imposed upon it. No freedom was lost. Indeed, this quality has spilled over into a degree of liberty of usage characteristically British, and which is the wonder of overseas visitors pre-conditioned to the prohibitive notices of their own public gardens. The public is excluded from very few sections of the Royal Parks, and then only for some definite reason. Guard rails are kept to the minimum, because the grass is there to be used, as are most of the edges of ponds and lakes. There are exceptions, however, as in St James's Park where much of the lake's margin is railed off in the interests of the wildfowl population.

There are ten of these Royal Parks, with St James's Park and the Green Park separating Piccadilly from Westminster, and Hyde Park and Kensington Gardens forming a central stretch of greenery, flowerbeds, ornamental water and recreational areas bounded on three sides by Park Lane, Knightsbridge and the Bayswater Road. Of the other Royal Parks, Regent's Park has a less well-endowed sister in the form of Primrose Hill. Hampton Court Home Park and Bushy Park, separated effectively by a main road, have certain affinities, not the least of which is the fact that their attractions are overshadowed by the splendours of Hampton Court Palace and its lovely gardens. The result is that they are uncrowded, and of great amenity value. Greenwich Park, comparatively little known to visitors who become hypnotised by Thames-side Greenwich itself, is a microcosm containing all the essentials of a Royal Park. It is much appreciated by local people as well as by the green-starved population on both banks of the lower reaches of the river. And, if Greenwich Park is a microcosm, Richmond Park is the macrocosm, with its open spaces, wildlife and beautifully patterned woodlands. G. A. Jellicoe, writing authoritatively on landscape design, divides London parks into three categories: Richmond and Bushy Parks are termed natural; Greenwich, Kensington Gardens and Hampton Court classical/historical; Regent's Park and St James's romantic/ historical; while Hyde Park is cosmopolitan. Primrose Hill and the Green Park are omitted.

London, of course, has other open spaces. These are run by the Greater London Council, and are maintained by the ratepayers in the interests of the local urban population. In all, Inner London has 2½ acres of open space to 1,000 head of population. The Royal Parks are Crown Lands. As such, they have become a symbolic feature at the heart of the Commonwealth, epitomised by Hyde Park, with Speakers' Corner as a focal point. Not only are they used by Londoners of all ages and ranges of interest, but they are a recognised tourist attraction. British holiday-makers and foreign tourists throng the Royal Parks at all seasons. The space, peace and variety of sights come as a relief after the congested pavements, traffic-jammed and airless streets, and the crowds in shops and popular sightseeing Meccas. The abrupt transition is almost unbelievable to anyone not familiar with the density of London's living standards.

The Londoner himself has a unique involvement with the Royal Parks: he feels he owns them, even though the facts are otherwise. Some guidance as to his usage of these parks is to be obtained from a survey of the use of open spaces published by the Greater London Council Planning Department in September 1968, though these findings should be interpreted with reserve since the Royal Parks, which possess such peculiar identities and histories, were not included. But since they too are metropolitan public open spaces, many of the findings of the report

10

are applicable to them. The survey was in three parts, the first of which was based on home interviews of 2,015 adults living in thirty-three wards of the then County of London; these people answered questions on their usage of, and attitudes to, public open spaces. Secondly, actual users of thirteen parks were approached; thirdly, questions were put to children aged eleven to sixteen in London County Council schools. The information obtained was that the average number of visits to a park in each 1,000 of population was 1,040 per week, with adults engaged in further education and those owning dogs forming the largest groups. Seventy per cent of visits occurred between Monday and Friday, while weekend visitors tended to frequent the larger parks, travelled further and often in company, and spent a greater length of time there. By far the greatest number of people—86 per cent of the total—went to the parks to read, stroll around, sit or simply observe. Only a small minority —12 per cent or less—went for sports, entertainments or activities with their children. Parks over 300 acres had a catchment area of at least 5 miles, those of 150 acres of between 2 to 5 miles, those under 150 acres a mere ¾ mile. The Royal Parks are mostly of substantial acreage, especially where paired.

There is much in common between all ten Royal Parks, not only because they are historically linked by royal ownership, but because they are centrally administered by the Department of the Environment. However, it requires no very acute observation for a visitor to realise that each park jealously retains its own individuality. Each park or group of parks is under the care of its own superintendent, and the innate character of his territory affects his attitude to it, and consequently his judgement and taste. Ten parks: they might just as well be ten related individuals; though differing in age and upbringing, the genes are similar.

One of the secrets inherent in the persistent individuality of each park is that, though centrally administered, they do not necessarily share re-sources. In some cases, for instance, the supply of water necessary for lakes and ponds is self-sufficient; in others, water has to be piped in by the Metropolitan Water Board. Each park, or group, raises its own bedding-out plants, and may have a tree nursery. Regulations (kept to a minimum) vary from park to park, according to need. Closure hours differ. Primrose Hill, for instance, like the old Windmill Theatre, never shuts. Some parks, such as Bushy, which is run in the manner of a country estate, are self-supporting in terms of agricultural machinery. Richmond has specialist needs; it owns, for instance, a machine for breaking down bracken—a necessary operation where its growth may create a hazard by obstructing a motorist's field of vision. Smaller parks call in outside help from the Property Services Agency—the successor of the Ministry of Works Surveys Department—when there is heavy work to be done. Of the ten, St James's Park was the only one to be redesigned expressly for public use. Regent's Park lagged behind the others in admitting the public; at first access was limited to keyholders. The anomalies and discrepancies spread out into every field of activity, and therein lies the fascination and divergent identities of even those parks which for convenience are twinned.

One very important common factor should, however, be emphasised: every single member of the work force seems to be deeply concerned with environmental and ecological issues. As a result, here at least there exists one sphere which is minimally threatened by pollution and man's improvidence and ill-channelled manipulation of technology. Those responsible for the administration and physical management of the Royal Parks move slowly, but according to proven patterns. Experimentation is rarely attempted on any large scale, so that a cautious pilot scheme may go unremarked by the public unless outstanding success or failure results. Conventional, traditional, old-fashioned, reactionary, all these adjectives might be levelled against the Royal Parks policy. But that would be ignoring the result: the parks exist as havens rather than backwaters, but at least havens full of colour and activity, which achieve an atmosphere of permanence and peace by ignoring brash new trends and developments. The environment is safeguarded through common sense rather than ideology. Scum and lake weed are not removed by any of the many chemicals available on the market. Not only would they upset the biological balance of the lakes and ponds, and possibly add to the pollution of the Thames, but the practice could affect the deer which drink from them. Weedkillers are not used on the grass, since children must be free to roll about and put their fingers in their mouths. For the sake of the deer, too, motor-powered model boats are banned from many ponds. Leaves are collected in traditional leaf yards, so that humus may be returned to the soil. Birds and animals are protected, from kindred and human predators alike. Vandalism, and the more powerful pressures of urban growth are resisted to the fullest degree. Perhaps the greatest achievement of all is that here in the ten Royal Parks, nature can run an uneventful course in spite of being hedged about by excesses which cause grave concern to all thinking people.

Though many of the Royal Parks owe their existence to their association with palaces, it is beyond the scope of this book to describe these splendid buildings. The same applies to the Zoological Gardens in Regent's Park and the Maritime Museum at Greenwich. At the same time, park users cannot fail to be conscious of Hampton Court Palace, nor of the more modest Kensington Palace. Richmond and Greenwich palaces have gone; the Prince Regent's *guingette* envisaged by John Nash for Regent's Park was never built and St James's Park seems to have transferred allegiance from St James's Palace to Buckingham Palace. Detailed descriptions of these buildings, and of museums and institutions closely related to the parks would extend this book into several volumes. Further facts and information can be obtained in many of the works listed in the bibliography at the end of this book.

Much has been written about the history of each park, together with anecdotes of personalities, protests, extravaganzas and tragedies. It is all there for the reading. The purpose of this book is to use historical events to delve below the somewhat complacent and conventional surface which the Royal Parks have presented through the centuries, in order to discover something of the well-oiled, silent machinery operating them through an unobtrusive array of workers; also to look at such items as design, water supply, trees and flowers, birds, beasts, entertainments and threats to their traditional character.

The Royal Parks of London

1 Primrose Hill
2 Regents Park
3 Hyde Park
4 Kensington Gardens
5 Green Park
6 St James's Park
7 Richmond Park
8 Bushy Park
9 Hampton Court Park
10 Greenwich Park

1

HYDE PARK

Though Hyde Park is all things to all people, it manages to preserve a sturdy individuality and has never lost its atmosphere of immunity from external pressures. Its fringes are crowded; Hyde Park itself seldom seems so, except in certain localised sections and at predictable times, such as Speakers' Corner on a Sunday afternoon and the Lido in high summer. And yet the park is not only prominent on the tourist map, but part and parcel of the everyday life of London's citizens. A worldly atmosphere, a balance between activity and restfulness, sets it far apart from its fellows, and distinct even from Kensington Gardens, from which it is physically separated by nothing more than a line of iron railings and a flow of traffic.

Originally Hyde Park was much larger than its present 360 acres for, as described in the next chapter, it included much of what is now Kensington Gardens. The northern boundary of Hyde Park was established during Roman times by the Via Trinobantium, which ran from Hampshire to the East Anglian coast, and is now the Bayswater Road. To the east the primeval forest was bounded by old Watling Street on its course from Dover to Chester, while to the south there was a third road intervening between what became market gardens and the swampy ground which carried the outflow of several minor streams into the Thames. Only the western boundary was arbitrary and it was from this quarter that Hyde Park suffered in the eighteenth century by having a substantial area filched from it for the benefit of Kensington Palace. Though the entire area was primeval forest, this was tamed many centuries ago. Nowadays open spaces intersected by straight paths and well ordered avenues near its edges are essential characteristics of the whole, which is broken by the artificial Serpentine, which widens below

Kensington Gardens' Long Water and Rennie's nineteenth-century bridge, which is one link between the two parks.

Because of the variety of amenities it incorporates, The Park—none other, not St James's, Regent's nor Green Park is thus familiarly designated—is difficult to describe. To those who know it well, different areas are associated with different breeds of users. The park's staff, or the police with their specialised spheres of interest, could possibly map out distinct areas, rather in the same manner as ornithologists are able to define the exact territories of birds in a garden. In proximity to Marble Arch, they say, you might find vagrants, the meths drinkers and those who are addicted to a mixture of cheap red wine and cider. Then there are a few shady hundreds of yards most favoured for homosexual encounters; in the Cockpit, the elderly sit in their deckchairs and read or knit, just far enough removed from the constant passage of feet along the northern edge of the Serpentine. The teenagers and young adults seem to prefer to slump themselves down on level ground at a little distance from Marble Arch. Others are variously disposed: patient fishermen in the area of the Serpentine allocated to them; the Americans playing softball; the riders of Rotten Row and the West and North Carriage Drives, blissfully disobeying all the obsolete canons of orthodox dress; the oarsmen and the sailing enthusiasts; the intrepid bathers; the staid bowls players; the walkers who come for the exercise and fresh air, or for athletic training, or quite simply to admire the flowers. But above all, the attraction is people, other people, and few regular park users would agree with Billy Graham, the American evangelist, in his diatribe against the parks: 'the lungs of London are becoming the Lust of London'.

Naturally it is people within a historical context who have determined the uses to which different sections of the park are put. Records range from the mid-tenth century, when St Dunstan was Bishop of London. About a hundred years later this portion of 'the Manor of Eia' was bestowed on Geoffrey de Mandeville as reward for his services at the Battle of Hastings. He subsequently bequeathed the land to the monastery of St Peter in Westminster, in order that it be used as the 'lardour' of the monks—a pious wish which argues the land's productivity. In exchange the Norman knight was granted the privilege of burial within the Abbey of Westminster.

As with the majority of Crown Lands, the property was sequestered by Henry VIII in 1536 when 'His Most Royal Majesty was desirous to have the games of hare, partridge, pheasant and heron preserved in and about the honour of his Palace of Westminster for his own disport and pleasure.' He thus acquired 'the syte, soil, circuyte and precyncte of the Manor of Hyde [Eia]' from the Abbot of Westminster, giving in exchange the Berkshire priory of Hurley.

In those days crown hunting lands were of three kinds: forests, chases and parks. A forest was a tract of country where hunting rights were exclusive to the king, and where a special code of law was enforced by an army of verderers, agistors, foresters and woodwards. A chase was unenclosed, but was governed by civic law and supervised by keepers and woodwards. A park, though similar to a chase in respect of the enforcement of law, was invariably enclosed by walls or palings. Henry VIII made sure that the newly acquired manor lands should fall into this third and most jealously protected category. At the time of acquisition, the lands spread over 620 acres, and because the park was then dedicated to the chase, agriculture declined to vanishing point. Hawking was popular, and streams were crossed by the use of vaulting poles. Poachers were prosecuted to the extremity of the law—which meant death. Elizabeth I carried on the tradition of hunting and entertaining in the Royal Park, by staging many military displays and lavish banquets aimed at impressing visiting monarchs and their emissaries as to the style and puissance of the State. Many of these occasions are well documented in the *Hatfield Papers*. John Norden confirms in 1592 that Hyde Park was 'substantially impayled with a fayre lodge and princelye stands therein'.

Public admittance to the park was granted in the reign of James I, who was always on the lookout for some means of alleviating his unpopularity. From that reign onward, popular festivities reached their height each May Day, and were concentrated principally around the Lodge, the refreshment place near the centre of the park, north of the water which was to become the Serpentine. Otherwise known as the Cake House,

Mince Pie House and later Cheesecake House, this was the forerunner of Charles Forte's establishments in the park. During the Civil War the park was temporarily closed and fortified against potential Royalist attack. Under Commonwealth rule, the whole of Hyde Park was disposed of in three lots to private purchasers, and in 1652 the deer were sold by parliamentary resolution, the proceeds being allocated to the Navy.

Happily, immediately following the Restoration the sales of Crown Lands were nullified, the new owners being recompensed. The newly appointed ranger, James Hamilton, then recommended restocking the park with deer, and confined them inside a high brick wall not far from the present Buck Hill Walk. The last royal shoot was staged on 9 September 1768, when there was a 'Diversion of Deer Shooting' for the benefit of visiting princes.

With Charles II taking personal interest in the parks within such easy reach of his palace, it is not surprising that Hyde Park became the resort of fashionable and sycophantic individuals, as well as of the spellbound masses who followed in the train of their 'betters'. The diaries of John Evelyn (1620–1706) and Samuel Pepys (1633–1703) give vivid pictures of Society converging daily upon the Ring, which consisted of two concentric carriage tracks with a contrary traffic flow, so that the participants could both see and be seen. Here Lady Castlemaine, the notorious one-time Barbara Palmer and future Duchess of Cleveland, could sometimes be glimpsed 'lying impudently upon her back, asleep' in her carriage, or 'ogling the King, or driving in yellow satin with a pinner on'. The fashionable round was liable to be brought to a halt for as much as an hour when the lovers commanded their horses to be reined in, for a period of dalliance. The Ring, which was probably near the present police station, where several paths now converge, was destroyed in the eighteenth century by excavations and drainage work when the lake was being constructed.

William and Mary, during their reign, put in fewer public appearances than their pleasure-loving predecessors. They preferred the seclusion of Kensington Palace and Hampton Court, and appear not to have concerned themselves overmuch with the unrefined goings-on of Hyde

Park, particularly amongst customers partaking of refreshment at the Cake House. The refreshment rooms of the period bore some resemblance to a modern drive-in milkbar in the United States, though with a lower standard of behaviour. An eyewitness reports a bevy of ladies partaking of refreshments brought to their coaches. Some were 'singing, others laughing, others tickling one another, and all of them Toying and devouring Cheese Cakes, Marchpane and China Oranges'.

However, standards of decorum were introduced in Queen Anne's day. She issued rules of conduct aimed at abating the nuisance. No hackney coach, chaise with one horse, cart, waggon or funeral cortège was allowed to pass through the park, and no one was to cut or lop any of its trees. Riding on slopes or near the edges of the ponds was prohibited. More tellingly, gatekeepers were banned from selling liquor. All these regulations were aimed at excluding the unrulier elements amongst Londoners, as much as dampening their exuberance.

The reintroduction of human peacock-displays had to wait until the 1770s, during the reign of George III. The *Westminster Gazette* then criticised men of fashion: 'The men imitate the women in almost everything. Perfumes, paint, and effeminate baubles engross most of their time, and now learning is looked on as an unworthy attainment.' On one occasion a guards officer went so far as to wear, during military exercises, a white frock coat lavishly ornamented with gold cord, over a waistcoat and breeches of blue satin. He contrived to keep the offending smell of gunpowder from his nostrils by the use of a scented handkerchief. To make matters worse, the 'degenerate and unmanly practice' of partaking of Tchai or tea in silken tents and pavilions was making its insidious attack upon the virility of commissioned officers.

In the 1730s a major threat to Hyde Park and Kensington Gardens arose from the ambitions of Queen Caroline of Ansbach, the wife of George II. She had intended to build a huge palace inside the park, a scheme which would undoubtedly have involved resequestering as much as 300 acres of what was coming to be regarded as public property. However, she was prevented from committing such suicidal folly by the prime minister of the day, Sir Robert Walpole. When approached for his opinion as to the cost of the project, he gave her the laconic answer,

'No more than a Crown, Your Majesty.' But the threat to Hyde Park must have been real enough. A report in *Reeds Weekly Journal* or *British Gazetteer* of 26 September 1730 states baldly, 'Next Monday they begin upon the Serpentine River, and the Royal Mansion in Hyde Park; Mr Ripley is to build the House and Mr Jepherson to make the River under the Directions of Charles Withers Esqre.' At that time Withers held the position of Surveyor General of Woods and Forests. But though the queen had to content herself with Kensington Palace as her most central London residence, her wish to create a 'serpentine' stretch of water extending from near the Bayswater Road almost to the Knightsbridge boundary went ahead. The scheme had obtained the king's sanction, the proviso being that the queen should pay all costs out of her own pocket. He was to discover subsequently that the requisite £20,000 had in fact been advanced by Sir Robert Walpole out of Treasury funds. Nor did the new stretch of ornamental water conform to the queen's specification; far from being serpentine, despite the name that has stuck to it, the lake when completed was in the form of a single curve. Though the scheme was not completed until 1733, by May 1731, six months after the beginning of work, there was sufficient water for the launching of two royal yachts, the forerunners of the nylon-sailed boats which nowadays contribute so much to the scene. A touch of fantasy was added by swarms of tortoises, the gift of the Doge of Genoa.

Previously, during the reign of William and Mary, when that asthmatic king and his queen had been installed permanently in Kensington Palace, removed from the fumes and bad air of the metropolis to the east, it became necessary to safeguard communications between the village of Kensington and St James's by creating a carriage road, then known as the King's Road, on the south side of the park. As a miraculous innovation, the new road was lit by a series of 300 lanterns —the earliest known instance of public street lighting in England. Rotten Row was created some four decades later. In more senses than one it runs parallel to the Serpentine, because whereas Queen Caroline created the lake, it was her husband, George II, who made the carriageway—not so successfully, though, because its surface was so bad that there were many accidents, one of them being a spill involving four of the royal princesses. Nevertheless, it is accepted that the name given to the king's ride did not refer to its condition, but was an anglicised version of *route du roi*. The drive is first mentioned in an issue of the *London Spy Revived* of 1737: 'The King's Road . . . is almost gravelled and finished, and lamp-posts are fixed up. It will soon be levelled and the old road levelled with the Park.' The old road referred to is what is known as the South Carriage Drive, the King's Road built by William III for safe and rapid transit. Nevertheless, although communications between St James's and Kensington were vastly improved, full security could not be guaranteed. In particular, during the reign of George III the park was haunted by highwaymen and footpads, so that it became necessary for travellers to and from the village of Kensington to be summoned by bell before being convoyed along the dangerous route.

It was during George III's reign, too, that Hyde Park acquired increased notoriety as a duelling ground. Though challenges to single combat in the park had been known since Henry VIII's days, when two peers of the realm fought each other with swords and bucklers, formalised duelling was not to become *de rigueur* until the eighteenth century, brought about, it was said, by the prevailing decline in morals. *The Gentleman's Magazine* of February 1750 reports what must have been one of the first of these encounters, though one year later the custom appears to have been in full swing, at least according to Henry Fielding in *Amelia*, where he describes duelling 'at that Place which may properly be called the Field of Blood, being that part a little to the Left of the Ring, which Heroes have chosen for the Scene of their Exit out of this World'. Affairs of so-called honour conducted ritualistically in the park are also vividly described by Thackeray, Defoe and Swift. It is recorded that during the sixty-year reign of George III, 172 duels were fought in Hyde Park. In three cases both duellists were killed, while there were sixty-three fatalities among the remainder.

In line with Hyde Park's transition from being a royal monopoly, equipped for entertainment of the Court and its guests, into open spaces for the use of Londoners, pageants and junketings on the grand scale were promoted from early in the nineteenth century under, it need hardly be said, the auspices of the Prince Regent. The Jubilee Fair of

1814, which fulfilled the dual purpose of celebrating the end of the Napoleonic Wars and the centenary of the accession of George I, outrivalled comparable displays in St James's and the Green Park. Sports, popular entertainments and firework displays proliferated, but all else was transcended by the glorious 'Naumachia', an enactment of the Battle of the Nile. The only criticism of this pageantry was that it was severely restricted by being staged on the circumscribed waters of the Serpentine. Again, in 1821—this time to mark the coronation of George IV—the pageantry reached a climax of absurdity in the presentation of elephants ridden by 'oriental slaves' on rafts disguised as chariots, which were towed by rowing boats the length of the Serpentine. The water was ornamental indeed, enhanced as it was by countless Chinese lanterns and an illuminated temple surmounted by a magnificent crown—the one the new king had waited so impatiently to wear. The evening ended with more fireworks, the climax being a set piece depicting George IV in a triumphal chariot drawn by a white horse. Brighton had come to London.

Fashions generally, and fashions in entertainment, followed the lead of royalty. Those manners which nowadays are labelled as Victorian prevailed soon enough in Hyde Park, through which the young queen and her consort drove daily between five and seven in the evening. Ladies dressed modestly, and gentlemen were not permitted to smoke when in feminine company, for fear of offending susceptibilities. There was no lack of entertainment during the celebration of Queen Victoria's Golden Jubilee in 1887, and a contemporary newspaper reports the 'joyous laughter of the people, untouched by debauchery and unseduced by the gross pleasures of the appetite'. On this occasion the amusements took up as much as one-third of the park, and the upper classes felt secure enough to alight from their carriages to join condescendingly in the fun. Also in celebration of her Golden Jubilee, the queen gave a treat to 26,000 schoolchildren, on the north side of the park. Another large-scale Victorian festivity was 'Peace Rejoicing', the 1856 fair which marked the end of the Crimean War. But the most illustrious achievement of all was the Great Exhibition of 1851.

This ambitious project was foreshadowed by the Society of Arts

Exhibition of Manufactures in 1847. Prince Albert, as president of the society, assumed personal responsibility for a successive scheme when it was mooted in 1849. An extract from the minutes of a meeting of the society held at Buckingham Palace on 30 June records that:

> His Royal Highness communicated his views regarding the forma-
> tion of a Great Collection of Works of Industry and Art in London
> in 1851, for the purpose of exhibition, and of competition and en-
> couragement.
> His Royal Highness considered that such Collection and Exhibition
> should consist of the following divisions:
> > Raw Materials
> > Machinery and Mechanical Inventions
> > Manufactures
> > Sculpture and Plastic Art generally.

In the January of the following year a Royal Commission was appointed

> to make full and diligent inquiry into the best mode by which the
> production of our Colonies, and of foreign countries may be intro-
> duced into our Kingdom; as respects the most suitable site for the
> Exhibition; the general conduct of the said Exhibition; and also the
> best mode of determining the prizes, and of securing the most
> impartial distribution of them.

Alternative sites were canvassed, but eventually the Prince Consort's choice was adopted: an area inside the southern boundary of Hyde Park, opposite Rutland Gate. Contemporary newspaper reports, particularly those dealing with the possible destruction of the park's trees, make excellent reading. The opposing forces were headed by a firebrand member of parliament with the imposing name of Colonel Charles de Laet Sibthorp.

The greatest inspiration of all came from the ultimate choice of designer: Joseph Paxton, creator of a gigantic greenhouse in his capacity as gardener to the Duke of Devonshire at Chatsworth. The result was the splendid structure of glass and metal which came to be known as the Crystal Palace. The first iron column of this revolutionary building was erected on 26 September 1850, and the work was completed by 1 May 1851. The area covered was approximately eighteen acres, and the principal building's dimensions were 1,850 feet by 408 feet and 64 feet high, without taking into account the roof of the transept. Frontages for display ran to ten miles. The intention was to accommodate 40,000 visitors at any one time, but in the event this number was swelled to 100,000. Written into the contract was the stipulation that the site should be cleared seven months after the close of the exhibition. This was done, and the entire structure dismantled and re-erected at Sydenham. In the 1930s Osbert Sitwell advocated its return to Hyde Park, but the idea received no support, and the Crystal Palace was in fact destroyed by fire in 1936.

Sport and popular entertainment, military reviews and social encounters, and even this unique demonstration of international and imperial achievement reveal only certain facets of Hyde Park. It had darker and more serious undertones which run like threads through its history. Most notorious feature of all was the Tyburn Tree, the gallows which for centuries stood at the north-eastern corner of the park. The exact location is debatable, though an iron plate was set into the ground to mark its most authenticated position. At any rate, the guesswork may be narrowed down to within a few hundred yards of the Edgware Road and Cumberland Gate; 49 Connaught Square has its adherents, other authorities favour the public house in the Edgware Road. The gallows consisted of an equilateral triangular structure made of poles, standing twelve feet high, each side accommodating eight malefactors. Hangings were a public spectacle, and as an incentive to informers Tyburn Tickets were issued to successful prosecutors of felons. These tickets could be resold, in the manner of Cup Final tickets, and are known to have fetched as much as £280 apiece. The practice was discontinued in 1818. Famous events include the execution of Perkin Warbeck in 1499; the public penance done by Queen Henrietta Maria, wife of Charles I, in expatiation of the blood of martyrs shed there; and the hanging of the exhumed bodies of Cromwell, Ireton and Bradshaw on 30 January 1661.

But traumatic memories of Tyburn Tree have now been dissipated, perhaps not so much by the passage of time as by the inexorable flow of heavy traffic which has critically affected the Marble Arch corner of the park. Marble Arch itself, made to Nash's design, discarded from its original position as an entrance to Buckingham Palace then re-erected here is marooned, purposeless and greatly diminished in scale, as well as now being outside the park's boundaries as redrawn in concession to the Park Lane traffic development scheme. However, the authorities responsible for this major upheaval knew better than to abolish nearby Speakers' Corner, the impromptu forum renowned as one of the major places in the world where free speech may be practised. As such, it joins the Tower of London and the Changing of the Guard as a major tourist attraction, as well as providing a constant source of free entertainment for Londoners. Crazy, provocative, earnest, pathetic—almost every epithet except 'dangerous' may be tagged on to the speakers who range from members of the Black Power movement, Communism, Gay Lib, Zionism, the anti-Apartheid movement, Evangelism, through the complete gamut of minority grievances. It is a valuable outlet for passions and rarely inflammatory. It took the Irish question—long debated here —to overturn official tolerance. In June 1972 two men appeared at Marlborough Street court on charges of sedition, the allegation being that 'on March 19th, 1972, at Speakers' Corner, Hyde Park, in the hearing of liege subjects of Her Majesty the Queen they did utter seditious speech inviting people living in London to go to Northern Ireland to take up arms against lawful authority'. Charges were also preferred against a third individual for inciting people in London to train as soldiers to fight in Ulster. Following remand in custody, the accused were tried in January 1973 at the Old Bailey, and though the main charges were dropped, were given suspended sentences for belonging to a para-military organisation. In the words of one defence counsel, 'If this trial does anything it will put to sleep any myths that might have grown up about there being a hallowed tradition of free speech at Speakers' Corner.'

But this police action is exceptional. Protests, demonstrations and soapbox oratory overlap, and do much to fill what might otherwise be written off as a dreary English Sunday afternoon.

But though Speakers' Corner and its vicinity was for many years the maelstrom of disturbance, invective and, at the least, unmannerly behaviour, by far the greater portion of the park continued to enjoy high social prestige and patronage. Fashions fluctuated: at certain periods the aristocracy frequented the South Carriage Drive west of Hyde Park Corner. Then the Wellington Drive to Marble Arch took over. Edward, Prince of Wales, excluded by Queen Victoria from participating in State affairs, spent much of his time riding in Rotten Row. And Lily Langtry, one of the most famous of his mistresses, attracted all eyes. She wrote, 'If I went for a walk in the Park and stopped for a minute to admire the flowers, people ran after me in droves, staring at me out of countenance, and even lifting my sunshade to satisfy their curiosity.' After Edward VII's accession, Queen Alexandra regularly drove round the park between six and seven o'clock in a high C-spring barouche with red wheels. Nowadays, the police stationed in Hyde Park are kept advised of the movements of royalty, for instance to and from Kensington Palace, as well as those of foreign ambassadors, so that the necessary security precautions may be taken.

Gradually over the years there was less social demarcation, though it was recognised that prayer books were an obligatory accessory for church parade beneath the trees bordering Rotten Row. But formerly, and possibly it is so even now, it was tacitly acknowledged that the bandstand concerts, not far from Hyde Park Corner, were for the masses—a term which did not include members of the upper or sophisticated classes. These days, of course, there are few noticeable social distinctions, either in regard to the dress or manner of the people, or in the areas they choose to frequent. Nor can there be threat of daytime closure of the park, except in times of national emergency, as when food dumps were set up in the park during the General Strike of 1926, and when in the last war barrage balloons floated sublimely above the park's plane trees. During World War I and World War II, it was considered necessary to dig trenches and shelters in Hyde Park. But when peace eventually came again, the park took on the role that the Crown and our legislators throughout the centuries have ensured it should fulfil—of being the very quintessence of a People's Park.

2

KENSINGTON GARDENS

The fact that Kensington Gardens and Hyde Park are poles apart in style and atmosphere is all the more strange because they interlock like two pieces of a jigsaw puzzle. In fact, the 275 acres of Kensington Gardens as we know them now were taken from the westerly side of Hyde Park, for the purpose, originally, of creating select gardens and grounds associated with Kensington Palace. The present-day distinction between the two parks is emphasised by Kensington Gardens having no traffic at all within its boundaries, whereas Hyde Park is ringed by internal thoroughfares which relieve the congestion of the roads outside its perimeter. Nor does Kensington Gardens lend itself to extrovert gatherings, being frequented by habitual users who come alone or in small units, and who appear to be satisfied to rely upon their own resources. Except for the bandstand, the conventional children's playground, and the Serpentine Art Gallery—striking a false note with the modernity of its exhibits, though not its exterior—there is little provision for popular entertainment. This does not imply that Kensington Gardens is without vitality or distinction.

The park was created in the landscaping styles of the late seventeenth and eighteenth centuries, and though it gradually departed from the rigid formality of other royal gardens, as instanced by Hampton Court, the fundamental features of such design are still discernable. Of these, the Broad Walk, which at one time may have formed the easterly limit of the palace gardens proper, has suffered most. Almost a mile long, fifty feet broad, and running directly north from Palace Gate to the Bayswater Road, its grievous loss has been the felling of its original elm trees in a devastating but necessary operation in 1953 and 1954. However, the new young Norway maples and sycamores flanked by sweet-

27

smelling limes, though slow to mature and not yet providing the shade which is one of the great virtues of avenues, will eventually bring beauty and comfort to succeeding generations of visitors. Some of the other avenues are less obvious, having been partially obliterated by time, but the design as a whole can be appreciated from a viewpoint where lines of trees and straight paths converge upon the giant Physical Energy statue, midway between the Round Pond and the Long Water.

As regards people in the park, it is the very young who immediately spring to mind; this being the traditional haunt of the English nannie and her charges. In fact the early memories of very many present-day Kensington, Bayswater and Notting Hill dwellers are likely to include the perhaps monotonous experience of having been trundled the length of the Broad Walk, or anchored in their perambulators while their elders (*au pairs* are ousting the starched nannies) met friends and sat and gossiped while enjoying the kaleidoscope of the Flower Walk. This attractive area, contrived out of an old gravel pit which provided ready-made elevations and shelter, realises the ideals of park horticulture by providing a succession of colour throughout the year in a blend of annuals and perennials, flowering shrubs and ornamental trees. For a later stage in the life of a child, there is the Elfin Oak in the children's playground at the north-western corner of the gardens. This is basically a gnarled tree-stump brought from Richmond Park in 1928, after which its natural crevices and convolutions were fashioned by Ivor Innes, the artist, into a proliferation of whimsical Little People, furred and feathered friends, and familiar objects from nursery rhymes. One wonders whether it should not be updated by the addition of a monster or two, a Dalek or strip-cartoon character, because its popularity seems to be on the wane. Not so Peter Pan, who retains his timeless enchantment and groups of admirers. The statue is satisfyingly integrated with the everyday life of the birds of the Long Water, many of whom have discovered better conditions for nesting here than on the shores or islands of the Serpentine, below the bridge which marks the boundary between the two parks.

But people of all ages make full use of Kensington Gardens. A fair sample invariably gathers around the Round Pond, which is enlivened by model boat enthusiasts of all ages, sailing anything from the simplest of home-made or mass-produced toys to expensive radio-controlled craft. At one time the Round Pond narrowly escaped being planted with overhanging trees; this would severely have interfered with the present combination of participant and onlooker sport, though perhaps the ducks, who manage to exist there on another level of enjoyment, might have had a greater share. However, they and some migrant visitors come into their own early in the morning and towards evening. Not far away, making use of open stretches of grass, there are usually to be found members of the kite-flying fraternity—again of all ages, but equally serious about what many regard as a science rather than a game. Beside the Kensington Road people throng to inspect the detail of the Albert Memorial, opposite the Albert Hall.

Although, historically, Kensington Gardens is indivisible from Kensington Palace on its western boundary, nowadays not every park user appreciates the connection between the two. For the origins of both it is necessary to go back to 1690, when William III bought Nottingham House from the Lord Chancellor, Heneage Finch, for £18,000, that price including twenty-six acres of garden. It seems expensive according to the then prevailing standards, especially in view of John Evelyn's denigration of the property as 'a patched up building with gardens'. In point of fact, it was the space which appealed to the king. He was asthmatic, and preferred the salubrious air of Kensington village to the pollution inseparable from the urban districts adjoining St James's Palace. That it was a patched-up building had little significance: Sir Christopher Wren was immediately commissioned to add another floor, to the tune of £60,000, and he it was who undertook restoration and further additions after a disastrous fire in the autumn of the following year, from which the royal occupants barely (perhaps literally) escaped with their lives.

When Queen Anne came to the throne she enlarged the Dutch gardens created by William and Mary, took in thirty acres of parkland, and enclosed her demesne with a haha or sunken fence in order that there would be no interruption to the vistas from her palace windows. She built the Orangery in 1704. It contains statuary which suits it well

29

enough, but why, oh why, is such a lovely purpose-built structure not used for growing oranges, so beautiful in sight and scent? Queen Anne is also responsible for planting the attractive mushroom-shaped hawthorn trees, which complement the scale and style of the palace.

But it was Queen Caroline, the wife of George II, who made the greatest impact on the royal property by bereaving Hyde Park of a further 200 acres and thus establishing the present boundary between the two parks, the northern section of which runs unexpectedly east of Buck Hill Walk, quite a distance from the Long Water, as the Kensington Gardens section of the Serpentine is called. Queen Caroline and her husband disliked 'old-fashioned' formality translated into straight paths, terraces and topiary; the clipped hedges of their inherited Kensington Gardens, said to have represented formations at the siege of Troy, were not tolerated. The Round Pond came into being. Both parks proved a suitable habitat for imported red squirrels, which managed to survive until the early half of the present century. Deer continued to be kept in the Kensington Park enclosure, and foxes were hunted there as late as 1798.

The reigns of the four first Georges were in some respects the heyday of Kensington Gardens, though for most of that time there was little benefit to the citizens of London. Public use had to wait until the 1790s, in the reign of George III, when the Court moved to Richmond Palace, and royal privacy would no longer be threatened by the common people. Even then, however, the gardens were open on Sundays only, and at all times were barred to soldiers, sailors and liveried servants. The enforcement of a high standard of dress and deportment was delegated to the gatekeepers, whose job it was to keep the 'great unwashed' at bay. Though early in the nineteenth century the gardens were open all week from spring to autumn, it was not until Queen Victoria came to the throne that admission was allowed throughout the year, though still restricted to respectably clad persons. The young queen, of course, knew Kensington Gardens well, having been born in the palace in 1819, spent her girlhood there, and been allowed to ride about on a donkey, sedately escorted. She must surely have approved of the Pets' Cemetery, founded by the Duke of Cambridge in 1800. This miniscule attraction takes a little searching out from behind Victoria Gate Lodge on the Bayswater Road. It is a strange, sentimental, comic or evocative place, depending upon how you regard manifestations of a past so near as not to be historic, but far enough, in terms of generations, as to be almost incomprehensible. At any rate, here are innumerable tiny graves, many with headstones and epitaphs, all worth studying. Ginger Blyth, of Westbourne Terrace, was 'a King of Pussies . . . whose little life was rounded with a sleep'. One Bondy, a Pekinese who died in 1949, has a commemorative marble cross. Others have Bible texts. Then there is dear Minnie 'of courage, sense and beauty rare—most loving and beloved', and Minikin, her daughter. Nigger, Prince, Yum Yum, these are predictable names, but what was Chip Wyatt? There is also Little Mab, who died on 24 January 1898, and was expected to give her owner 'joyous greeting at the Golden Gate'. One of the last burials was in 1953, of Kim, a Blue Persian cat. The small graveyard was then filled to overflowing. It is left to the occupant of the gate lodge to maintain the plot, which some people might consider to be as typically English as Speakers' Corner.

It was by Victoria's wish, late in her reign, that several of the State Apartments of the palace were put on view to the public, including the rooms associated with her birth and girlhood and with the dramatic announcement of her accession to the throne. For the pleasure of all comers there is also the separate Orangery, and glimpses of the lovely private sunken garden through squints cut for that express purpose in the pleached lime walks which surround it. These days the palace contains grace and favour apartments, among whose occupants are Princess Margaret, Lord Snowdon and their family. Also, since its removal from Lancaster House, Kensington Palace has housed the London Museum with its enthralling series of exhibits illustrating the history of London, some dating from more than 2,000 years ago. This museum, however, is due to close in 1974, previous to its establishment in the following year on a site at the corner of London Wall and Aldersgate in the Barbican (not far from St Paul's Cathedral), where it will be amalgamated with the Guildhall Museum. The two will then go by the name of the Museum of London. Beyond, outside the grounds, is that select resi-

31

dential street known as Millionaires' Row, which should these days be rechristened Ambassadorial Avenue.

But in spite of some modern changes, it is not unduly fanciful, when observing the contrasts between the two parks, to wonder fleetingly whether something of Queen Victoria lingers on in Kensington Gardens on each side of the Long Water. Certainly anyone seen there is usually 'respectably dressed' in line with a voluntary standard of conventionality not always adopted in the more popular and populous Hyde Park.

Page 33   *St James's Park:* (above) *View of 'The Canal' in 1813;* (below) *the park excels in lakeside walks for modern city dwellers*

Page 34 *Regent's Park*: (above) *The Holme, designed by Decimus Burton for his father;* (below) *the boating lake has its moments of peace*

3

ST JAMES'S PARK

St James's is the most garden-like of all London's Royal Parks. The irregular lake, the meandering paths, the informally grouped trees and flowerbeds and, incidentally, the prospect of the domes, spires and minarets of Whitehall are the work of John Nash. Though his architecture tended towards the grand classic style, his reconstruction of the park was based upon a determination, shared with Repton, to rid English parks and gardens of the rigid French formality which had reached its zenith in the work of Le Nôtre for Louis XIV.

What is now a ninety-three acre park was originally little more than a marshy tract liable to flooding from the Thames by spring tides. Heavily wooded land stretched to the north and west but water, or stagnant dampness, was the principal and most unpleasant characteristic, especially in the neighbourhood of the Cowford Pool into which the Tyburn drained. This was the location considered to be eminently suitable for the foundation of a hospice for fourteen poor sisters, 'maidens that were leprous, there to live chastely and honestly in divine service'. They were granted about 160 acres, which they farmed so diligently that they were able to extend their estate. A five-day fair was inaugurated by Edward I in 1290, to be held annually on the Feast of St James, in what was then known as St James's Field. After deduction of expenses the proceeds went to the hospice.

But when Henry VIII took up residence in Westminster, he objected to the proximity of the dismal hospice in its sodden grounds. In 1530 he was able to do a deal with Eton College, the nuns' administrators, by granting certain East Anglian lands in exchange. Similarly, the king acquired a further hundred acres from the Abbot and Convent of Westminster, this time giving them a Berkshire priory in compensation. The transactions were completed in 1532, making this the first of the London parks to be designated 'Royal'. The newly acquired lands were thereupon enclosed by 'a sumptuous wall of brick' and an existent manor house became the nucleus of St James's Palace. In other unspecified ways the king 'devised and ordained many singular and commodious things, pleasures, and other necessaries, most apt and convenient to appertain only to so noble a prince, for his singular comfort, pastime and solace'.

A plan of Westminster, drawn by Norden in 1593 in the last decade of the reign of Elizabeth I, shows a large circular pond at the west end of the park, with rivulets branching from it. This was known as Rosamond's Pond, though the origin of the name is obscure. The remainder of the park was open grassland, with an avenue and orchard near the Privy Gardens of the palace. There was a deer harbour, and sufficient fish and waterfowl to justify the appointment of Keeper of the Ponds in the Park of Westminster in 1572.

The land remained uncultivated during the reign of James I. The Stuart king had a passion for wild animals, and he installed a menagerie in the park. His beasts included one 'ellefant' sent to him from Spain by his favourite, Buckingham; hawks and sables presented by the Czar of Muscovy; antelopes from the Great Mogul, and a leopard from the King of Savoy. Crocodiles were accommodated in ponds near the Vine Garden attached to the palace. There were also fishing cormorants. The annual upkeep of the elephant amounted to £273, a figure which did not take into account the daily gallon of wine which was considered essential for its well-being—or that of its attendant.

A visitor in 1638 emphasises the pastoral nature of the park, which was at that time well 'planted with divers avenues of trees, and covered with the shade of an innumerable number of oaks, who old age renders them very agreeable, as it makes them impervious to the beams of the sun'. It was through this bosky and allegedly dark park that Charles I was escorted in 1649 from St James's Palace to his execution at the Banqueting House in Whitehall.

In 1652, under the Commonwealth, St James's Park was exempted from the general order for the sale of Crown Lands. The deer must have disappeared by that date, because the park had to be restocked from Hampton Court and Bushy at a cost of £300. This sum was taken from funds received from the sale of the deer from Hyde Park, a typically wasteful bureaucratic transaction, since a simple transfer of beasts from one park to its neighbour would have been more logical. During most of this period the park was closed to the general public, though the world of fashion continued to have access, and in particular the houses backing on to the park retained their rights of usage.

Great changes came about with the Restoration. It is generally accepted that Charles II brought Le Nôtre over from France as a consultant for St James's Park, but that this great landscape gardener refused the assignment on the grounds that the rustic simplicity of the site would not lend itself to any superimposed formal scheme such as graced the palaces and châteaux of France. However, in spite of this setback, Charles II went ahead with plans which were largely based on the French style which he had admired during his exile. According to Samuel Pepys, as early as September 1660, 300 workmen were already employed in connecting the various pools, which then made a continuous sheet of water, a hundred feet by twenty-eight feet, which came to be known as the Canal.

At that time the game of pall mall was in vogue. The improvised playing alley had been moved from the then dusty thoroughfare to which its name has been given, and a ground, 1,424 feet long, was created on the site of the present Mall. It was spread with pulverised cockle shells, making a fast surface, and a man known as a cockle strewer was employed to maintain it. Along one side there was an avenue of elms, used by coaches, and over the way one of lime trees, for pedestrians. A pheasantry was situated on the present site of Marlborough House. The park was opened to the people in the first year of the Restoration.

During his reign Charles II walked regularly in his park, without fear of moving among his subjects. One of his pleasures was the feeding of the birds and beasts kept on the original Duck Island, many of whose wildfowl had been lured into captivity by decoys installed in the reign of James I. In February 1664, John Evelyn mentions seeing a 'pellican—a

37

fowl between a stork and a swan, a melancholy waterfowl, brought from Astracan by the Russian Ambassador'. There were also 'two Balearan cranes, one of which having had one of his legs broken and cut off above the knee, had a wooden or boxen leg and thigh, with a joint so accurately made that the creature could walk and use it as well as if it had been natural'. The breeding of wildfowl in the park he considered to be an achievement 'which for being near so great a city, and among such a concourse of soldiers and people, is a singular and diverting thing'. There were also withy pots or nests woven out of willow. These were placed some height above the surface of the water, making safe places for the parent birds to produce their young. Many of these Carolean practices are still continued on present-day Duck Island; but what we do not see now are the harboured deer, or the wild beasts and exotic birds which are thought to have been exhibited in cages along what is now known as Birdcage Walk. Yet it is strange that no contemporary prints depict them. Food for the birds is recorded as having cost as much as £246 18s od for the nine months ending June 1670—presumably there must have been some misappropriation. At that time Duck Island was small, and intersected by numerous channels. The pond keeper was paid £30 a year. He undertook all the routine but rewarding work such as is at present done by the birdkeeper, and presumably was not interfered with when the king jocularly created one of his courtiers the 'Governor of Duck Island'.

Skating became a craze during this reign, the pastime having been imported by the king from Holland, after the years of his exile. Pepys, that indefatigable social climber, reports on 15 December 1662 that he went to 'the Duke [of York] and followed him in the Park, when, though the ice was broken, he would slide upon his skates, which I did not like; but he slides very well'. But skating did not in fact become a widely practised sport, for Swift, writing to Stella in 1711 complained that 'the Canal and Rosamond's Pond [were] full of rabble and with skates, if you know what that is'. In any case the creation of the Serpentine in 1736 superseded the waters of St James's for this winter sport.

William III was of a contemplative, indeed phlegmatic, disposition.

He indulged no more than was necessary in blood sports, and preferred to be an observer of nature. He built himself a small house on Duck Island to act as a hide. Seasonal flooding continued to be a hazard, and a terrific storm in 1703, after the accession of Queen Anne, uprooted more than a hundred elms, thought to have been planted in the reign of Henry VIII. The park, which was now open to the public, became the resort of the fashionable world who, however, considered it vulgar to sit on benches, so that this unseemly practice was left to members of the lower classes. Of greater importance was the fact that since St James's Park existed in such close relation to the royal court, there was no right of arrest within its boundaries, except in the case of treason. Nor were swords allowed to be drawn in the park. These interdictions should have guaranteed that St James's Park would be a peaceful place, but in fact vandalism and the terrorism of gang warfare plagued the area. That the offenders were young men of rank, labelling themselves as Mins, Nickers, Mohawks and such names, does not take the edge off the comparison with modern urban violence.

During the reign of the first Hanoverians, coaches were not permitted to be driven through St James's Park without authorisation. In fact sometime earlier Sarah, Duchess of Marlborough, had been outraged when as a sign of her fall from favour with Queen Anne, the privilege was withdrawn from her. Actually, the boorish George I took scant interest in the park at his doorstep, and is accused of having considered growing turnips there. At least the suggestion gave fodder to his Jacobite critics. Beyond reviewing his troops there, George I used the park infrequently. In fact, he was seldom seen by his subjects. Judging from contemporary plays, in those days the parks appear to have been socially notorious rather than fashionable.

With the accession of George II there was some improvement: the king and Queen Caroline walked along the Mall, which was the one part of the park to remain well kept, still by the practice of rolling cockle shells into it. And for a brief period the fashionable world amused itself by parading in an expensive parody of the artless graces of shepherds and shepherdesses. The amenity value of St James's Park had come to be critically affected by its bad condition until, in 1733, the

39

deputy ranger successfully petitioned the Board of Works to put it into repair. Some attempt was then made to improve Rosamond's Pond, which had been the scene of a drowning on a foggy night, when two sedan chairmen accidently tipped their lady passenger into the water. They it was who drowned; the lady was saved. The pond received further attention three years later, when it was drained and cleaned out by a miraculous engine which was claimed to be capable of sucking out thirty tons of water a minute. For many years the pond had held romantic associations, of equal notoriety as a trysting place and as the ultimate sanctuary where unrequited lovers could, literally, drown their sorrows. The new works now made it unsuitable for either purpose.

At this time the park was remarkable as the scene for the settling of preposterous wagers. It was nothing to see a man running naked from point to point, or an infant crawling on all fours the whole length of the Mall. Many and various were diversions of this type. Queen Caroline, too, showed humour in appointing a strange character named Stephen Duck to be governor of Duck Island. This man, a corn thresher turned poet, eventually took holy orders and, being of a melancholy disposition, finally drowned himself, but elsewhere. In the autumn of 1736 a large army bivouac was established in St James's Park, as a precaution against riots which were expected to follow government restrictions on the sale of gin. About the same time Hogarth, most celebrated for his talent as a social and political caricaturist, frequented the park in search of archetypes for his bawdy pictures of fast life. Similarly the dramatists and literary celebrities of the era used the park as a background for many of their satiric comedies. It is known, too, that Hogarth painted two 'straight' views of Rosamond's Pond.

By 1764 plans were again afoot for the park's improvement. These were to include the draining and filling in of the pond. However all that was done was the substitution of iron railings for the park's outer wall. Then a terrible storm occurred in 1768, bringing with it extensive flood damage. The result was that the Canal had to be banked with brickwork, and that 'shameful nuisance', Rosamond's Pond, was at last filled in, while the moat around Duck Island, notorious for its stagnant water and thickets of willows and brambles, was also condemned. The work

40

was completed in 1770. One unfortunate environmental consequence was that a great number of marginal trees died within a year of the completion of the drainage scheme.

St James's Park remained countrified. Much of it still consisted of grass plots where milkwomen grazed their cows at a charge of 2s 6d, later raised to 3s, a week. Twice daily these four-legged dairies were driven towards Whitehall, where their milk fetched 1d a mug. Nothing much of importance happened in the park during this period, though a military encampment of 4,000 soldiers in 1780 temporarily destroyed its amenity value. However, some attempt at providing comfort was made in 1785, when an indigent but enterprising gentleman introduced chairs, whose hard wooden seats were padded with 'elastic' cushions. These, at least, were socially acceptable.

Extrovert pleasure was to come to St James's Park in 1814, with the Jubilee Fête which celebrated the centenary of the House of Brunswick. The festivities were planned to be more select than those of the adjoining Green Park. Accordingly a fee was charged for admission to an area embracing Birdcage Walk, the Parade and much of the space facing Buckingham Palace. John Nash threw a parody of Venice's Rialto Bridge across the Canal, embellishing it with a splendid Chinese pagoda. Illuminations were the in-thing, gaslight being a novelty. Unfortunately towards the end of an exuberant fireworks display the elegant structure caught fire, five of its storeys fell into the water, and several workmen were killed or injured. Nevertheless the festivities lasted a whole week longer, during which time the public were allowed full and free use of the lawns and the Canal.

It was in January 1827 that Nash was called in to undertake a permanent transformation of the Royal Park, with the result that it is the only one to have been expressly planned for public use. The design was part of his only partially realised plans for a processional way leading from a fully developed, and economically viable, Regent's Park to Carlton House and the open space beyond. To break the formal pattern once and for all, the straight Canal was converted into a lake with irregular margins and an island at each end. The lower one was named Duck Island after its predecessor. Nash's bridge across the lake, however, had to be replaced in 1857, and once again a hundred years later, the modern designer being Eric Bedford.

During World War II the lake was drained, to prevent its becoming a landmark for enemy bombers aiming at the destruction of Westminster's political and economic nerve-centres and Buckingham Palace. The park itself was blemished by the temporary buildings of government offices.

It is largely due to Nash that Buckingham Palace has become such a focal point and link between the Green Park and St James's Park. The Mall leads to the enormous roundabout, with the Victoria Memorial at its centre, where the flowers are predominantly bright royal scarlet, providing a glorious splash of colour facing the palace itself. In point of fact, it is nearby St James's Palace which is the official headquarters of the Crown, although not nowadays a residence of the sovereign and the royal family. And it can be argued that the older palace suits St James's Park better than the more pretentious and massive complex attempted by John Nash in the period of his decline in reputation, and subsequently altered. As it is, Buckingham Palace might be criticised for being in direct contrast in appearance and atmosphere to the central parks which Disraeli praised by saying that 'in exactly ten minutes it is in the power of every man to free himself from the tumult of the world'. It takes the office workers of Victoria Street, and the civil servants of Whitehall, less time than that to reach a lunchtime nirvana.

4

THE GREEN PARK

Because of its uniformity, which amounts almost to featurelessness, the Green Park gives the illusion that it is flat. Equally there is no justification for an eighteenth-century account of Constitution Hill as, 'a pleasing ascent to one of the finest eminences of Nature!' A more realistic description would be a heavily wooded, triangular area, with a dip between two shallow hills, the higher ground lying to the west. The thirty-six acres added to St James's Park by Charles II have now been increased to fifty-three, and make it a park in its own right. Piccadilly bounds it to the north; Constitution Hill, between Hyde Park Corner and the main entrance to Buckingham Palace, forms its southern boundary; and at the eastern end the park is overlooked by a range of what were once great houses and gardens extending from the Ritz Hotel to Lancaster House, and without access for traffic from the park side.

It is not known how or when the park came by its present name. Researchers have failed to identify some ranger or keeper of the name of Green and the most obvious of all explanations must be accepted. Closely planted trees are one characteristic of this area which acts as a valuable breathing space and lunchtime resort, but which perhaps is of greatest importance as an undeveloped link between Hyde Park and St James's Park.

Though there is water available for all necessary purposes, it feeds no grand ornamental basin or pond. Formerly a stagnant pool of water collected in the dip, and was probably connected with a rivulet from the Tyburn. Sir Robert Peel had dreamed of formal terraces with stonework and statuary, but nothing came of the idea, and it is on record that Lord Palmerston objected to the use of iron hurdles in the park, expressing the modern view that the grass was intended to be walked upon freely and without restraint by the people, old and young, for whose enjoyment the parks were maintained. Apart from this swampy pool, there existed until 1855, near the Piccadilly boundary, a large reservoir holding 1,500,000 gallons of water.

In search of features, mention must be made of the Broad Walk, the purpose of which is to provide Piccadilly with a vista of the Victoria Memorial at the centre of the approach to Buckingham Palace. Otherwise there is the Queen's Walk, running parallel to the eastern boundary, which is much used as a direct line of communication with the bandstand and St James's Park, as well as having some historical significance. Though the original trees in the park were principally willow and poplar in the damper areas, and oak and ash on the higher ground, there is now greater variety, though nothing exotic or ornamental has been introduced. Similarly, there are no flowerbeds, though the bulbs set in the grass inside the northern railings, west of Green Park tube station, make a fine display in spring. But though the Green Park is the least dramatic of London's Royal Parks, its history contains almost orgiastic episodes of national peril, revelry and catastrophe.

Until Charles II's restoration in 1660, what is now the Green Park was meadowland, not very heavily wooded, used solely as grazing. The area had come into prominence in 1554, when it was fortified and manned by loyal supporters of Queen Mary led by the Earl of Pembroke in order to resist the anticipated attack by Sir Thomas Wyatt and his Kentish adherents, who aimed at forcing Mary to marry an Englishman in preference to the Roman Catholic Philip of Spain. The rival forces clashed south of Hay Hill, just north of what is now Piccadilly. Wyatt was taken prisoner, and executed on Tower Hill on 11 April 1554. Less than one century later, in 1643, a cordon of forts was constructed by the Parliamentarians, together with a small redoubt and battery on Constitution Hill. This time the object was to menace Charles I in his palace of St James's.

When Charles II returned to the throne, one of his interests was the replanning of St James's Park. Upper St James's Park, later to become the Green Park, was part of the grander undertaking. Strype, in his continuation of Stow's writings records that, 'St James' Park hath been much improved and enlarged, by King Charles II, having purchased several fields, which ran up to the road as far as Hyde Park, now enclosed by a brick wall.' The wall in question is known to have cost £2,400. Previously, an ice house and a snow house had been built at a central point, and these stood until the early nineteenth century; in fact, the foundations of the latter may still be identified opposite 119 Piccadilly. Previous to King Charles's development, the trees of what had been open land were mainly concentrated at the south-eastern corner; but now large-scale planting was undertaken in conjunction with a network of gravelled paths. A harbour for deer was constructed near Hyde Park Corner and, it is said, Constitution Hill received its name at that time because the king was in the habit of taking a daily therapeutic 'constitutional' along that route, accompanied by his spaniels. These, and other royal 'walk-abouts' amongst his subjects, were an unheard-of practice and very dangerous, but in this, as in many other respects, the king went his own way.

In 1689, the year of the accession of William and Mary, some land to the east was granted to the Earl of Arlington. Though in the following years the Green Park acquired a reputation as a convenient duelling place, there now ensued a fundamentally quiet period in its history until Queen Caroline, wife of George II, became interested in it. According to the *London Journal* of 21 February 1730 the Board of Works was at that time ordered to provide a private walk in Upper St James's Park for the queen and the royal family 'to divert themselves in the spring'. The result was the already mentioned Queen's Walk, close to the eastern limit of the park. The queen's intention had been to build a small minor residence off the walk, but the idea got no further than the creation of the Queen's Library. This was less a library in the accepted sense than a summerhouse for reading and other sedentary pleasures, but the project was ill-fated, and possibly contributed to the queen's death since she caught cold when walking to it for breakfast on 9 November 1737, and died ten days later. The building was accidentally set on fire and destroyed by crowds celebrating the Peace of Aix la Chapelle in 1749.

Other improvements were made in 1730. The northern boundary was

45

partially railed, replacing existent brickwork, the object being to open up a fine view over Pimlico towards Surrey. In that year, too, considerable alterations were made to the Ranger's Lodge. A contemporary critic carps: 'The Ranger's House has been recently altered and enlarged but has acquired no beauty by that means. The enormity of balcony which environs it looks like the outriggers of an Indian canoe, to prevent it from oversetting.' There is no opportunity for testing the witticism; the lodge was demolished in 1842, when the basin erroneously known as Rosamond's Pond was filled in, and the ranger's gardens were incorporated into the park. At that time the Green Park was in constant demand for those 'military evolutions' which are nowadays banned in most of the Royal Parks.

During the reign of George II the Green Park was chosen for spectacular celebration of the end of the War of the Austrian Succession. The idea was to erect a colossal Temple of Peace as the focus of attention. It has been described by Larwood:

The building was intended for a Doric Temple, 114 feet high and 410 long, covered with frets, gilding, lustres, artificial flowers, inscriptions, and allegorical pictures, besides 23 statues all of a colossal size. The great picture on the pediment in the centre was not less than 28 feet by 10, and represented His Majesty giving peace to Britannia. On the top was a gigantic sun which was to burn for four hours [and] an infinity of fireworks was to be let off from this rococo construction.

A temporary gallery equipped with a bridge was constructed for the use of the royal visitors, and the outer park walls were breached in order to let the crowds through. In spite of reverses—the designer fell ill before completion, and his deputy was severely injured—the project continued inexorably towards what was to be both opening night and disaster on 27 April 1749. The performance began with a grand military overture on the theme of war and peace, commissioned from Handel. The 'barbarous band' was composed of 40 trumpets, 20 French horns, 16 hautboys, 16 bassoons, 8 kettledrums, 12 sidedrums and a 'proper number' of fifes augmented by 100 cannon planned 'to go off singly with the music'. Unfortunately the whole box of tricks caught fire within 1½ hours of the royal party's arrival, perhaps because of the huge number and variety of the fireworks, which included 'tourbillions, pots d'aigrettes, pots de brin to the number of 12,000, cascades, vertical suns and wheels, lances, maroons, etc., all of Italian manufacture'. The cost to the nation was £90,000.

Until what by hindsight appears to be a repeat performance, the Green Park then enjoyed a period of high-level social renascence in contrast to St James's Park, which was frequented by all sections of the public. By about 1790 not only was the Queen's Walk fashionable, but the 'shore' of the reservoir, owned by the Chelsea Waterworks, became the venue for parades of the *ton*, elegantly dressed in all the extravagance of the period. Then came 1 August 1814, in the heyday of the Regency, with Jubilee celebrations to mark jointly the centenary of the House of Brunswick and victory over Napoleon. The area designated for the festivities covered one-third of the entire park, and its centrepiece was to be a Temple of Concord, a magnificent construction in the form of a 'Gothick' castle, sited near Constitution Hill. The walls and ramparts were plastered with allegorical pictures depicting the whole pantheon of heroes and British virtues which had contributed to the overthrow of the French emperor. These telling representations were backed up by fireworks, gunfire, rocketry and illuminated ornamentation on every conceivable surface, making up over two hours of confused imagery, but culminating in metamorphosis from Siege to Victorious Peace. However, two things contributed to popular disappointment amounting to bathos. The festivities were scheduled to begin after dark, and the crowds, impatient at being temporarily barred from the park, were drawn away by the sight of the Chinese pagoda on the bridge across St James's Park lake in flames. Then, though a bridge had been specially constructed for the processional arrival of the Prince Regent, he did not condescend to put in an appearance. Whatever the cause, next day the Temple of Concord was nothing more than a charred skeleton. Someone inserted a satirical advertisement in a London newspaper:

Lost, on Monday night, the beautiful Green Park, which used to extend from St James's Park to Piccadilly. It is supposed to have been removed by Mr John Bull, who was seen there last night at a pretty numerous party, and who has left a Brown Park in exchange, of no value, to the Ranger.

To make matters even worse, for at least another fortnight the park was afflicted by an epidemic of vandalism by a public infuriated at being given no further outlet for their high spirits on the occasion of the Prince Regent's birthday. To add to these disasters, the park had been used by horsemen and carriages as a short cut between festivities in Hyde Park and St James's Park, with the result that the turf was reduced to a quagmire. For as long as two months the charred skeleton of the Temple of Concord remained standing amid scenes of riot, outrage and drunkenness. Then what remained was sold in a hundred lots for a total of £198 6s 6d.

It was not surprising that the coronation of George IV in 1821 was marked by a less rabble-rousing festivity—a balloon ascent by an aptly named Mr Green, who drifted off serenely towards a landing at Potters Bar. However, even then there was disaster: the crowd, feeling cheated of excitement, surged towards Hyde Park to see the regatta taking place there, and ran into a bottleneck on Constitution Hill. The casualties were high.

Celebrations to mark the end of World War II were even less spectacular, though a great many deckchairs were set alight.

5

REGENT'S PARK AND PRIMROSE HILL

Though Henry VIII appropriated the lands which became known as Marybone or Mary-le-bone Park as hunting grounds conveniently close to his residence in Westminster, present-day Regent's Park shows no evidence of this phase of its development. Unlike the other Royal Parks in and about London, whose limits are drawn with some regard to topographical features, this one is almost circular. Its outline, in fact, cut through all existing manorial boundaries, so that it is possible that the king drew an arbitrary circle on a map, and acquisition then began. The owners of the land either accepted payment or compensation in the form of alternative property at the royal disposal. The transactions were probably made easier by the fact that the locality consisted almost entirely of pasture and woodlands, and contained no buildings of account, with the exception of the Tudor manor house which stood near York Gate and was demolished in 1791. Hindsight reveals that two features dictated the eventual aspect of Regent's Park: its essentially pastoral character made for an easy transition into leasehold farmland when hunting was discontinued and, more obviously, its shape presented John Nash with a ready-made ground-plan for the most northerly section of his great Regency town-planning scheme nearly 300 years after the date of enclosure.

Initially Marylebone Park was contained by a ring mound, was stocked with deer and provided with gamekeepers' lodges. Edward VI maintained interest in the new hunting grounds, protecting his game from poachers, and conducting water to bricklined ponds for use by the deer. However, soon after her marriage to Philip of Spain, the young king's successor, his elder half-sister Mary, contemplated

dissolving the Parkes of Maribone and Hyde and having bestowed
the dere and pale of the same to their Majestie's use, upon a due
surveye of the grounds of the said Parkes so as to distribute the
parcelles thereof to the inhabitantes dwelling thereaboutes, as may
be most to their Highnes' advauncement and commoditie of their
loving subjects.

In spite of approval by the Privy Council, nothing came of the project,
and when Elizabeth I came to the throne she followed the example of
her father by once more using the park for hunting and lavish entertainment.

Financial troubles forced Charles I to mortgage the park to two of his
supporters who had lent him money to help meet the expenses of the
Civil War, and similar measures were adopted by the Commonwealth
Parliament, except that under its régime the land was divided into
smaller parcels and allotted to a greater number of tenants. To this end,
and in common with other Crown Lands, Marylebone Park was sur-
veyed and assessed in 1649. It was scheduled as comprising 534 acres
containing 124 deer worth £130 and 16,297 trees, of which some 3,000
were to be reserved for the Navy. Felling began in the following year,
and the deer were removed in January 1651. It is clear that by the time
Charles II was restored to the throne almost all the remaining trees had
been felled and their roots grubbed up by tenant farmers who had converted their holdings into pasture for cattle. The situation was ideal for
dairying, to supply the growing city to the south and east.

Marylebone Park now diverged from other London Crown Lands. It
was never restored to its previous state, nor at any early date was opened
to the public, but continued as leasehold property on a shifting pattern
of occupancy, the only consistency being that the lands were farmed in
conjunction with properties lying outside its boundaries, so that the
perimeter fence ceased to have relevance. As urban transport problems
grew, hay became the principal crop, outweighing even dairy produce.

Meanwhile, beginning with the accession of Queen Anne, Acts of
Parliament were passed restraining the sale of Crown Lands and re-
stricting leases to periods of thirty-one years. Until George III exchanged

Page 51 *Hyde Park*: (above) *Near Grosvenor Gate, a busy meeting place for London society in the nineteenth century; (below left) on the fringe of Speakers' Corner; (below right) and when the crowds have gone. . . .*

Page 52 *Greenwich Park*: (above) *The splendid indestructible view from the park, taken from a nineteenth-century print;* (below) *the old Royal Observatory*

revenues from these for an annuity from the Civil List, the income was allotted to the royal household. Marylebone Park then became the subject of successive surveys by three commissioners appointed by Parliament. The most effective and visionary of these men was John Fordyce, who was the first to realise the park's potentialities for urban expansion. Leases had been renewed in 1772, and upon the death of the major lessee in 1789 the remainder of the lease of Marylebone Farm was sold by auction to the Duke of Portland, who already owned extensive property to the north-west, as well as a whole district centred around what is now Portland Place. One of Fordyce's first moves was to oppose the duke's request for a turnpike road to be driven straight through the park, since he considered that such a project would depreciate the value of land ripe for development. His next move was to promote a competition open to architects and designers, inviting them to produce a comprehensive development scheme. The result was three entries, all by John White, a surveyor who worked for the Duke of Portland. Though the award was never made, and though Fordyce died before his dream of 'a great scheme from Charing Cross towards a central part of Marylebone Park' could be realised, the ideas of both men were assimilated by John Nash under the enlightened patronage of the Prince Regent.

The idea of public competition having been abandoned, Nash, as official Architect and Surveyor of Woods and Forests, submitted plans to his master in 1811, the year of the expiration of the Duke of Portland's lease. The advantage of his plans over all earlier submissions was that economics and aesthetics were given equal value. The scheme had escalated to one in which the Prince Regent would be provided with a processional way beginning in the park and leading by way of Portland Place and Regent Street to Westminster and which, by the development of adjacent properties, was calculated to recover its cost. In so far as the pilot scheme of Marylebone Park was concerned, the benefit seemed obvious. The proposition was that an outlay of £12,115 would result in capital appreciation to the astronomical figure of £187,724, from which a substantial annual income could be derived. The royal estate was to be provided with houses and buildings which would be likely to 'assure a great augmentation of Revenue to the Crown', and the

D

amenities generally should act as 'allurements or motives for the wealthy part of the Public to establish themselves there'. One important feature of the scheme was that the principal approach was to be from the south, thus shutting off all unnecessary contact with districts which had already become slums. In fact, what at drawing-board stage was renamed Regent's Park was to be a select and self-contained housing estate originally of twenty-six, later containing fifty-six, villas imaginatively sited so that each one appeared to own the whole park. But what was to give Regent's Park its individuality was the ring of palatial terraces in neo-classical style, whose stucco façades would mask houses which, though expensive, would be well within the means of worthy lessees. The design also fitted in with the canal to the north, a commercial undertaking upon which Nash was already engaged. And, to appeal to his patron, the most important of all the inner park's buildings was to be a *guingette* or pavilion for the Prince Regent's personal pleasure. Thus Nash's scheme deployed all his talents as planner, property developer, designer of genius and human being imbued with an understanding of his patron.

The story of this aspect of the creation of Regent's Park is a long one, complicated by financial considerations which ran counter to all possibility of complete accomplishment—as early as 1816, Nash's estimate had risen from £12,115 to over £53,650. The solution was found by dividing the park into building sites upon which speculators were invited to erect houses which conformed externally to Nash's designs; ninety-nine-year leases were then granted on a ground-rent basis. The Office of Works was thereby relieved of financial responsibility, and public money was necessary only for roads, railings and similar amenities. What happened inside the park is inseparable from the perimeter development, and from the whole neighbourhood. Accounts of how Nash 'metamorphosised Mary-le-bone Park Farm and its cowsheds into a rural city of almost eastern magnificence' are to be found in the works of Sir John Summerson and Terence Davis.

Present-day frequenters of Regent's Park are understandably mainly concerned with its present-day appearance. The great terraces, bearing their weighty Hanoverian and ducal names, were realised over a period from 1812 (Park Crescent) to 1827 (Gloucester Gate), and act as a frame which many people consider surpasses the picture itself. However, the frontages, which were to Nash's design, excelled the interiors, which were not. From the first the latter were criticised as mean, unworthy and inapposite. Unfortunately, the terraces were extensively damaged in the air raids of World War II, so that for a time their future was at stake. St Marylebone Borough Council urged wholesale demolition and the use of the ground for 'multi-storey flats of mixed character'. But in 1962 the Crown Estate Commissioners authorised rebuilding of the original façades combined with a complete reshaping of the interiors, so as to make the terrace buildings economic, thus prolonging their expectation of life at least some distance into the twenty-first century. They established the principle 'that the present building line should be adhered to in perpetuity' and that any further building inside the park itself was to be deprecated.

The lake is another survival of the original design. In the words of a contemporary visiting prince:

faultless . . . is the landscape-gardening part of the park . . . especially in the disposition of the water. Art has here solved the difficult problem of concealing her operation under an appearance of unrestrained nature. You imagine you see a broad river flowing on through luxuriant banks, and going off in the distance several arms; while in fact you are looking upon a small piece of standing, though clear, water, created by art and labour.

In fact, the deliberate lack of formality displays the influence of Humphry Repton, who had partnered Nash from 1795 to 1802, and who is credited with being the first landscape gardener to develop an English style as opposed to the rigid geometrical patterns which had prevailed in France for many years.

The Inner and Outer Circles were important features in Nash's scheme. It may or may not be regrettable that the former was never provided with concentric terraces, to be named the Inner Circus and the Great Circus, which appear on the 1811 plan, and whose houses were intended to command a substantial income. Nowadays the Inner Circle is simply a road which rings what were the grounds of the Royal Botanic Society, and which are now Queen Mary's Gardens. This island site, completely screened from the road, except through the great grille of its main gates, has its own pretty little irregular lake, the artificially constructed Mound; internationally famous Rose Gardens; and the Open Air Theatre. The so-called Outer Circle, which carried a greater volume of traffic, has straight lengths running parallel with the park's boundaries, demonstrating that Henry VIII's sketch, if it ever existed, was by no means a perfect figure. At one point this carriageway runs between the tree-shaded Regent's Canal and the main grounds of the Royal Zoological Gardens.

Another modification of the original design came about with alterations to the Broad Walk near the eastern boundary of the park, inspired by the Prince Consort, who directed the creation of a flower garden and herbaceous border along its southern section, as well as the installation of giant granite urns which the park's nurseries—near at hand—manage to keep overflowing with flowers. Nash's intention at one stage had been to devote this part of the park to a continuation of the stately way from Portland Place, and central to the classic curves of Park Crescent; but the plan was never realised and the Broad Walk is now principally used by pedestrians hurrying to and from the Zoo. There is no sign, either, of the long strip of ornamental water which appeared on Nash's 1811 drawing, and which was to have been garnished, at its centre, by his fairytale palace for a Prince Charming who by that date had lost his comeliness and much of his charm and who, when at length he reached the throne, no longer had a taste or need for a metropolitan architectural conceit and was already concentrating with Nash on the more solid virtues of Buckingham Palace. The *guingette* was never built. Nor did the fifty-six villas ever materialise. Indeed, only six were built, and though a greater number would doubtless have added extra style, distinction and revenue to the Crown property, the present-day public may bless the omission in that, eventually, a more extensive acreage of open land was available for public recreation and enjoyment.

Two of the best of the original villas have survived, and are occupied by Bedford College, as part of London University. St John's Lodge was designed by John Raffield for the member of parliament for Sudbury, and the plans were exhibited in the Royal Academy of 1818. It is a charming, pedimented building which nowadays provides living accommodation for the principal of Bedford College and for post-graduate students. The lovely gardens, which are reached from its front, are open to the public. The Holme, also off the outer edge of the Inner Circle, was designed by Decimus Burton when he was only eighteen years old, for his father James, who was the most important of the speculative builders engaged in and about the new park. This villa was taken over in 1948, and is now a students' hostel. Bedford College itself has little to recommend it architecturally. It replaced South Villa—one of the early few—on a most attractive waterside site. Apart from the college's inappropriate architecture, its sprawl is to be deplored. The same criticism cannot be levelled against Winfield House, the residence of the US Ambassador, which was built for Barbara Hutton, the Woolworth heiress, on the site of Holford House, later St Dunstan's.

The history of the various leasehold properties inside and bordering the park is set out in Ann Saunders' *Regent's Park*, together with archi-tectural details and the all-important financial considerations. But though the letting policy is important, and shows how one Royal Park developed in a completely contrary direction from the other nine, it is important to realise that out of Regent's Park's 487 acres, 400 are now freely open to the public. This state of affairs was not easily stabilised. At an early stage it had been assumed that, as the occupants of the perimeter houses would not possess private gardens, the alternative must be to give them exclusive use of the grounds opposite their homes. For a period, therefore, the area between Hanover Terrace, Sussex Place, Cornwall Terrace and the lake was 'a subscription garden', much in the same way as many London squares are still reserved for the use of resident key-holders. The process of opening the park to the people was a gradual one: at first, only its roads were permitted to be used. Then, in 1833, a Select Committee on Public Walks represented that the small rents still derived from pasturage were insufficient to justify the closure of a large area, so that in 1835 much of the eastern part of the park and a strip bordering the canal—eighty-eight acres in all—was thrown open. In 1841, ninety-two more acres were similarly freed. It may be remembered that the official policy in relation to the Royal Parks is to restore ground to public usage on the expiration of leases. This practice came into its own during the between-the-wars period of economic recession. Many long-standing leases fell in during the 1920s, and though the Crown was prepared to renew them for twenty-one years at a higher rental, in many cases the offers were refused. The surrender in 1922 of the grounds occupied by the Toxophilite Society and those of the Royal Botanic Society in 1932 brought two large sections of the park into public use.

Though Primrose Hill is part of the domain of the superintendent of Regent's Park, these two Crown Lands have little else in common. Its 120 acres were not acquired by the Crown until 1841, by negotiation with Eton College, the owners, who readily exchanged them for land at Windsor. They were immediately made into a public park and, though on the map Primrose Hill seems to be an extension of Regent's Park, they are very effectively separated by the Zoo, the Regent's Canal and Prince Albert Road.

A current London guide book briefly notes 'a very minor Royal park of simple grassy hill 200ft giving a fine view over London', and indeed there is not a great deal more to be said. Six more feet could, for accuracy's sake, be added to the altitude, and in all honesty the view could be described as the very finest, and well worth the climb up that grassy hill or by a path with an easier gradient. The spread of London to the east, south and west can be seen in perspective—better for that reason than from the aerial viewpoint of the Post Office Tower which, from Primrose Hill, takes its place among the other landmarks. This is a natural site for a direction indicator or 'panorama', but its absence must not be blamed upon the authorities, since two have already been destroyed by vandals. So, regrettably without aid, the visitor will have to fend for himself in identifying such well-known landmarks as St Paul's Cathedral, the Houses of Parliament, Westminster Cathedral and the new tower blocks—hotels, offices and flats—which have recently been added to London's skyline. The difference is that from this vantage

58

point they do not punctuate the heavens, but settle into the cityscape in overlapping patterns.

There are no primroses on Primrose Hill, though its southern aspect should favour their early flowering. As it happens, representations were made by the Primrose League that some could appropriately be planted, but the request had to be refused, not on political grounds, but because they would have stood no chance against vandals.

It is an inescapable fact that this small and innocuous Royal Park has always attracted the unrulier elements of the local population. No attempt is made to close its gates at night, and though it is lighted by attractive old-fashioned lamps, these offer little safeguard. There can be no flower displays, except in the immediate vicinity of the gate lodge. A pond in the north-west sector was filled in in 1902, and the reclaimed ground was levelled to make more recreational space. The playground bordering Prince Albert Road is well patronised by children from the congested districts to the east. For the rest of the world, there is walking and a great feeling of space: grass and trees, trees and grass. And winter snow brings out the skiers and tobogganers. Also, it is rumoured, the hill is a favourite spot for 'gay weddings', though such occasions are outside the range of experience or taste of typical users of the Royal Parks. Better perhaps to return to the highest point, there to ruminate on the words of Mother Shipton, the Yorkshire soothsayer: 'When London surrounds Primrose Hill the streets of the Metropolis will run with blood.' Regent's Park and the Zoo are the last barrier.

6

RICHMOND PARK

Its 2,358 acres make Richmond by far the largest of London's Royal Parks. Irrationally, less than seventy of these acres are in the parish of Richmond, but because the principal approach is through Richmond Gate, at the top of the hill overlooking Richmond itself and the Thames valley, there is justification for the renaming of what was originally known as New Park.

This park conforms most truly to the traditional pattern of an English demesne: open stretches of grass, rough with bracken and grazed by deer; orderly coppices and spinneys and bigger plantations designed for posterity and landscape effect; grassy rides for horsemen and walkers, and nine artificial ponds which not only vary the scene but make convenient drinking places for the deer. Motor traffic is restricted to roads which, though some distance inside the perimeter, do not touch the heart of the park. The gravest environmental disturbance is in the thoroughfare between Richmond and Kingston gates, where the build-up of commuter traffic in rush hours is not only foreign to the spirit of the park, but is definitely hazardous. Cars may not be left at the roadside, but the special parking areas are sited not only to prevent their being an eyesore, but primarily to give access to the whole range of undulating high ground. The most striking individual features, to some eyes, are the giant oak trees, most of which are grotesque and 'stag-headed' or pollarded, an unusual practice for this type of tree. The explanation may be their use in earlier periods as a perennial and self-perpetuating source of fuel, though Edward Jesse, the Victorian naturalist and Deputy-Surveyor of the Royal Parks, believed that the branches had been cut at intervals as forage for the deer. Primeval is an adjective which springs to mind, and they are in fact scions of the forest trees which at one time encircled London.

The park is surrounded by a brick wall. Unfortunately its construction in the seventeenth century was so faulty that not much more than some re-used bricks remain from that period. What is missing is a great house, such as is usually associated with parkland—Thames-side Richmond Palace, completed in Henry VII's reign, fell into neglect during the Parliamentary régime. During Stuart and Hanoverian reigns, various cottages and lodges were converted, not only for the use of officials and employees concerned with the running of the park but also—and sometimes at great expense—for royal or otherwise privileged persons.

Some properties inside the park still go with jobs, as for instance White Ash Lodge, south of Sidmouth Wood, which is one of the oldest buildings, never having been rebuilt for the nobility. Its outbuildings were of greater importance than the cottage, because it was here that deer were slaughtered in times when they were farmed for food to grace the tables of the privileged. Two formerly important houses have vanished. The first, Old Lodge, was added to and improved during the rangership of Robert Walpole, second Earl of Orford, the cost being borne by his father, the prime minister. Later it became one home of Princess Amelia, daughter of George II, when she was appointed ranger. This house was demolished between 1839 and 1841. The second, Petersham Lodge, owned by the Hyde family, blood relations of Queen Anne, was burnt down in 1721, then rebuilt stylishly with colonnades each ending in a pavilion. It came into the possession of William IV when he was Duke of Clarence, but he sold it in 1833 to the commissioner of woods and forests, after which the house was pulled down, and its grounds added to Richmond Park.

Three of the largest properties inside the park are outstanding for their metamorphoses. The present White Lodge, originally Stone Lodge and later New Lodge (to distinguish it from Old Lodge) dates from 1727, when it was rebuilt as a hunting lodge for George II. It was in Portland stone, and had a huge banqueting hall. This country residence was much favoured by Queen Caroline, whose favourite walk came to be known as the Queen's Ride. Though Princess Amelia preferred Old Lodge, she sometimes stayed here. Two brick wings were added in 1767, during the rangership of Lord Bute. Though subsequently allowed to fall into disrepair, it was restored in 1801 by George III for Henry Addington, the prime minister who later became Lord Sidmouth and gave his name to Richmond Park's largest plantation. During his occupancy, some of the adjacent parkland was enclosed as private gardens. Humphry Repton made further alterations in 1816, and subsequently White Lodge went to the Duchess of Gloucester, who was ranger between 1844 and 1857. Later Queen Victoria stayed there, and at other times lent the house to members of the royal family. At one time it was the home of Princess Mary of Teck, who married George V, and was the birthplace of Prince Albert, who became Edward VIII. It is now occupied by the Royal Ballet School.

Thatched House Lodge derives its name from the thatched summerhouse constructed in 1727 and which was, *circa* 1780, provided with splendid ornate ceilings and walls painted by Angelica Kauffmann. The name is first recorded in 1771. It was here that Sir Robert Walpole, who had spent about £14,000 on this property, White Lodge and various smaller buildings, entertained royalty. The house was enlarged in the nineteenth century. From that time it has been a grace and favour residence, the present occupants being Princess Alexandra of Kent and her husband, Mr Angus Ogilvy. They are the only private persons living inside the park, apart from those whose houses are tied to their occupations.

The third notable house is Pembroke Lodge, built on the site of a molecatcher's cottage which existed until the mid-eighteenth century; that position having some prestige and responsibility because the safety of royal riders to hounds was at risk. When the cottage was transformed to become Hill Lodge, it was at first leased to the Countess of Pembroke, one of the beauties of George III's reign. She prevailed upon the king to present it to her, and lived there until her death in 1831. Only then did it acquire her name. Queen Victoria lent it to Lord John Russell, one of her prime ministers, and throughout that reign it continued to be a grace and favour residence. It now houses a restaurant and cafeteria, and the upper floors have been used as accommodation for the park's staff. There are beautiful gardens, and all-embracing views of the Thames valley.

Though impressive because of their length—nearly ten miles in circumference—Richmond's Park's walls cannot compare with those of Greenwich Park. But they possess one fascinating feature: an external freebord consisting of a strip of land measuring some sixteen and a half feet (one rod) which was kept clear for the convenience of workmen engaged upon the unremitting task of repairing the ill-constructed walls and because access from the park side was hampered by soft ground, as well as by the growth of brushwood which existed to prevent the deer from leaping through any breaches in the wall. The outer freebord boundary was partially hedged, to make a second obstacle to foil straying or hunted deer. The freebord was ritually patrolled or, in the language of the time, 'perambulated', by officers of the park. Nowadays the best maintained section of the freebord is near Ladderstile Gate, though it can be traced all around the boundary, except where it is discontinued for three-quarters of a mile on the Petersham edge of Sudbury Golf Course, on land formerly owned by the Marquess of Bute. Its existence has guaranteed that new buildings cannot be sited flush with the main boundaries.

Public access has always been an important issue. Of the six main entrances provided at the time of the park's enclosure by Charles I, Richmond Gate is the most important because it admits the heaviest traffic. Originally it was wooden, with a step-ladder—known as a ladderstile—for the use of pedestrians. The present imposing gates, erected in 1798, are attributed to Lancelot (Capability) Brown, and bear the royal cypher of King George III and Queen Charlotte. The remaining five of the original entrances are East Sheen Gate, Roehampton Gate, Robin Hood Gate, Ladderstile Gate and Ham Gate, none of which compares in beauty. A common factor, however, is that most of them are open to pedestrian traffic after nightfall, though subject to token annual closure in demonstration that pedestrian traffic is a matter of concession rather than right.

Richmond Park is well wooded, but except for the ancient oaks, most of the trees have been planted in neatly defined plantations. The reason

63

is obvious: deer and young trees are irreconcilable. Where access is denied to the public, the reason may be because the woodlands are bird sanctuaries, or because they have substantial newly-planted sections. As an example, the Sidmouth Plantation, largest of all, is fenced. It has a wide ride known as the Driftway forging through its centre, which was cut originally to afford a view of St Paul's Cathedral—and still does, given the right atmospheric conditions.

All that Richmond Park is today has come about principally by slow transition, and seldom by planning. Though Charles I was responsible for the enclosure and definition of the park much as it exists nowadays, the lands had been royal hunting grounds previous to the reign of Henry VIII. During the fifteenth century Sheen Chase and its immediate neighbourhood consisted of a combination of wooded Crown Lands, commons and derelict ground. Major changes did however occur in 1637 when Charles I, in the course of enlarging the grounds of Richmond Palace, created the enormous park on high ground above the Thames, and stocked it not only with common fallow deer but the larger red deer which would afford even better sport. The terrain was ideal for these animals. It had gorse for cover and was well wooded. Though this Stuart monarch is memorable for the high-handedness which led to his execution, in this instance he moved with a semblance of consideration for the rights of others. Not only were common lands involved, but a sizeable proportion of the land was privately owned, and six parishes were affected. Accordingly, a commission was appointed to make the necessary purchases, and though its terms of reference were to negotiate generous terms, some landowners resisted before eventually submitting to pressures which fell not far short of compulsion. Though the enclosure was not completed until 1637, two years previously the coveted acreage had been acquired from the manors of Ham, Petersham and Richmond, as well as from private landowners in the neighbouring parishes of Wimbledon, Putney and Mortlake.

Despite the circumspection employed throughout these dealings, local feeling ran high in those days of disenchantment with the divine right of kings. At first, however, Parliamentary opposition was chiefly directed against the cost of erecting such an extensive brick wall—a necessary measure for the preservation of game. However, Charles I was still all-powerful, and continued with his project, which he had initiated with the introduction of water, formation of ponds as drinking places, railing in of woodlands and turfing of rides. The New Park developed rapidly, and it is to the king's credit that, after paying high prices for the land, he guaranteed free communication between fringe towns by the provision of six gates and two rights of way, with ladderstiles placed against the walls for foot passengers. Poor people were permitted to gather firewood in the park. In fact, local people may still apply to the superintendent for a wood permit.

The king enjoyed his sport for a few years, and even during his imprisonment was permitted to hunt, the last recorded occasion being in the summer of 1647, two years before his execution. Though an Act was passed forthwith, directing the sale of Crown Lands, Richmond Park was excepted, in that it was presented to the 'Mayor and Commonalty and Citizens of London and their Successors for ever'. Difficulties arose almost immediately in respect of the park's trees. Parliament had reserved the right to use such timber as was necessary for the building and maintenance of ships of war, and was outraged to discover that the new civic owners proposed felling and selling trees. The objection was that it had been 'the intention of the Parliament in passing the Act for settling the new park at Richmond on the City of London that the same should be preserved as a Park still, without Destruction; and to remain as an Ornament to the City, and a Mark of Favour from the Parliament unto the said City'. The Court of Common Councill [sic] then issued an order safeguarding the park and the management of its game 'with the least charge to the Cittie'. Two salaried keepers were retained in office, and though certain farming and grazing rights were leased to them, the herds of 1,300 fallow deer and 200 red deer were maintained out of public funds.

Despite the patent enjoyment of Richmond Park by the city fathers, who incidentally used it as a source of venison for their official banquets, they deemed it politic to restore or 'present' the park to Charles II upon his return from exile abroad. In doing so they emphasised their new-found loyalty by declaring that when accepting Richmond from

65

Parliament they had regarded themselves as temporary stewards of the king's property. Charles accepted their explanation in gracious but cynical terms.

The office of ranger was revived in 1660, the first appointment being that of Sir Lionel Tollemache, Bt, of Ham House, and his wife, Elisabeth, Countess of Dysart. Substantial annual sums were provided for fodder for the deer, whose numbers, nevertheless, fell to a scandalously low figure by 1669. Five years later warrants were issued to private persons allowing them to dig and remove some 5,000 loads of gravel from the park. These excavations form the basis of most of the existent ponds and depressions. There was everlasting trouble with trespassing livestock, breaches in the walls and poaching which, in spite of dire penalties, it was impossible to suppress. Complaints were also made as to the poor standard of husbandry which produced inferior hay, while doing nothing to control the spread of rushes which strangled the growth of grass which might otherwise have been valuable. In 1674 the Receiver of Crown Revenues for the county of Surrey was given control of the park and its properties, without interference with the privileges of the ranger.

By the time Queen Anne came to the throne, her uncle, Laurence Hyde, first Earl of Rochester, was ranger and lived in Petersham Lodge. His niece conferred the office on the family for two succeeding generations. Though the Hyde family is held responsible for neglecting their duties, and were stigmatised by Horace Walpole for having allowed Richmond Park to relapse into 'a Bog and a Harbour for Deer-stealers and Vagabonds', they did at least show concern for the trees. On one occasion they protested against the felling of timber, even though it was for such a worthy purpose as the building of a chapel-at-ease on Kew Green. Once more they objected when in 1723 a royal warrant was issued for the sale of £2,000 worth of trees. On this occasion the protest was made by the second Earl of Rochester, on the grounds that the timber was of inferior quality, fit only for fuel, with a rider to the effect that the trees were ornamental rather than of commercial value.

Better times came during George II's reign, when the king bought the rangership back from the Hydes at a cost of £5,000. It was he who bestowed the office on Robert Walpole, the elder son of the prime minister of the same name. However, it was the father who effectively shouldered the responsibilities which accorded so well with his personal tastes including those already mentioned in connection with maintenance and improvements to properties, with much of the money involved coming from the family's private resources. There is a theory that the closure of the House of Commons on Saturdays originated with the prime minister's regular weekend retirement to Richmond Park, where gossip had it that his gamekeeper had better claim on his attention than any of his ministers.

Since during the reign of George II the White Lodge was used primarily as a hunting-box, particularly for shooting wild turkeys which had been introduced for that purpose, while the royal ladies and their female guests hunted from carriages, it is not surprising that measures were taken to limit the use of Richmond Park by the general public. The dates of royal hunts and shoots were kept secret, so as to ensure some privacy, and manned lodges were substituted for ladderstiles so that the respectability of visitors to the park might be scrutinised before they were admitted. Tickets were issued to privileged carriage owners, and as time went on further restrictions were imposed.

In 1747 Princess Amelia, the youngest daughter of George II, who already held office as Keeper and Paler of the House Park at Hampton Court and Manor of the Brakes, was additionally appointed Ranger of Richmond New Park in reversion after the death of Robert Walpole, who at that time was still officiating. She therefore did not take up the appointment until his death in 1751, in which year she removed from Hampton Court to Richmond Park. The princess introduced a further system of tickets by which even so-called 'respectable persons' were denied access as of right. Permits were in short supply, the idea being, of course, the preservation of game as well as the guarantee of royal privacy. But now public outcry began to be heard. The issue was fought in the courts with great acumen and perserverance by one John Lewis, a brewer, with the result that rights of way by ladders at East Sheen Gate and Ham Gate were confirmed. This means of entry was preferred to a

67

gate, which was capable of being closed and locked upon any pretext. The name of Ladderstile Gate on Kingston Hill is a reminder of early results in regaining at least limited use of the park for the general public. In the event, so popular was the legal decision, that the opening of the new ladderstiles in 1758 was attended by 'a vast concourse of people from all the neighbouring villages'. Shortly afterwards the scene was visited by one of the judges concerned in the legal action, and it was upon his recommendation that the ladderstiles were altered to bring the intervals between their steps within the range of children and old people. John Lewis died poor in 1792, and was buried in Richmond Parish Church. His epitaph recorded that by his 'steady Perseverance . . . the Right of a Free Passage through Richmond Park was recovered and established by the Laws of this Country (Notwithstanding very strongly opposed) after being upwards of twenty years withheld from the People'. Princess Amelia became disenchanted by these events. She gave up the White Lodge, where she had lived latterly, and eventually surrendered her rangership to George III in 1771 in exchange for an annuity of £1,200 to be paid from Irish revenues.

Further difficulties arose in 1793, when the dimensions of the freebord were challenged. When the king attempted to increase this peripheral strip by sixteen yards for the purpose of constructing a path, the scheme aroused the opposition of Richmond vestrymen, who pointed out to the 'perambulators' of the freebord that this could not be done without appropriation of parish land. This time, however, the popular movement met with minimal success: the parishioners were fobbed off by being granted the use of water from a pump and reservoir, and they accepted a peppercorn rent for their land.

During the nineteenth century good husbandry began to assume importance. Sheep and cattle were put to graze in the park, and in periods of food shortage, such as the Napoleonic and Crimean wars, land was put under the plough for wheat. A hundred acres of potatoes were grown near Sheen Gate in 1917 and 1918, and further crops sown during World War II. However, since the soil consists of London clay and gravel depressions, it is of greater value as pasture. A marked improvement in the quality of grassland was noticeable as soon as the

68

rabbit population came to be rated as vermin rather than game. Nowadays hay is the only crop considered to be worth growing.

The second decade of the nineteenth century saw the formation of well-defined coppices, planted and managed for their own sake and not exclusively as cover for game. Spankers Hill Wood and the Sidmouth and Isabella Plantations were fenced, the work being carried out under the enlightened direction of Viscount Sidmouth (Henry Addington) who, until his death in 1844, was deputy-ranger under Princess Elizabeth, sister of George IV. Seedling trees, delicate silver birches especially, stood a better chance of survival to maturity as soon as a system of phased planting was adopted, reinforced by secure fencing against the ravages of a herd of deer which was retained, increasingly, for ornament. The park was enlarged in 1834 by the incorporation of Petersham Lodge's 265 acres, though the house itself was demolished one year later. At about the same time the Terrace Walk from the stables of Pembroke Lodge to Richmond Gate was constructed, and though magnificent views of the Thames valley draw attention away from Richmond Park itself, this is one of the park's most memorable sights.

A drainage scheme covering some 1,378 acres was undertaken between 1856 and 1861 at a cost of £8,776, and was so effective in drying out swampy land that nine ponds had to be provided, mostly by the conversion of gravel pits, into watering places for deer and other livestock.

From 1792 to 1904 the rangership of Richmond Park had been held by members of the royal family, the majority of whom delegated the administrative work to their deputy-rangers. When the appointment fell vacant following the death of the Duke of Cambridge in 1904, King Edward VII assumed the office and reappointed a deputy-ranger, but entrusted the main responsibility for the park to the Commissioners of Works. This government department took over completely in 1910, relying upon the park superintendent and his staff for day-to-day management, much as is done today under the Department of the Environment.

E

7

HAMPTON COURT PARK AND BUSHY PARK

These Royal Parks have a distinct affinity despite there being no direct communication between the two, since they are separated by the busy Hampton to Kingston road, which with its verges makes a space known as 'Between the Walls'. Hampton Court Palace and its gardens stand a little aloof from the parks, in spite of being visually linked by the Long Water, a feature of the landscaping at the centre of radiating avenues which stretch out towards the River Thames. In all, these Crown Lands measure 1,785 acres of mainly flat, riparian land based on predominantly gravel soil. To break down this figure: Bushy Park has 1,099 acres; Hampton Court Park 615; Hampton Court Palace and Gardens 54; and Hampton Court Green, which also comes under the supervision of the Department of the Environment and the bailiff of the Royal Parks, a mere 17 acres. Originally the land was manorial pasture. Few of the trees are of natural growth; they are examples of planting on a grand scale. However, some hawthorns in Bushy Park give a fragmentary picture of what, previous to the sixteenth century, was mainly open heath. It has been suggested that these trees accounted for the name 'Bushy'. Those visitors with an eye for detail will observe that, as in Richmond Park, the trees of all descriptions tend to be bare of branches and foliage to a height of eight feet above the ground—the maximum reach of a full-grown stag.

Hampton Court Home Park falls into two sections: the area south of the Long Water known as The House Park, and the northern half, which contains the Stud House and the paddocks and outbuildings of the National Stud. This was originally called 'The Course', and it was here that the sport so greatly enjoyed by Henry VIII and Elizabeth I was staged. An interesting account of deer coursing in this park occurs

70

in the *Calendar of Domestic State Papers* for 1690-1. Bushy Park also was divided in the reign of Henry VIII, again in the interests of sport. There were three enclosures: the Upper Park to the west, Hare Warren to the east, and the Middle or Jockey Park lying between the two.

The Manor was sold in 1239 to the Knights Hospitallers of the Order of St John of Jerusalem in England, and in 1503 what was then no more than a manor house was used as an annexe to Richmond Palace while the latter was in course of reconstruction for Henry VIII. Later, in 1514, when Wolsey was Archbishop of York, but would have to wait one year more before he received a cardinal's hat, he acquired the tenancy under rather suspect conditions. In any event, the rapid elevation of that rapacious cleric required that he should be installed in palatial accommodation; a ninety-nine-year lease was negotiated at a price of £50 per annum and the manor house became a palace. As soon as he took up residence Wolsey came to the conclusion that there were insufficient facilities for stag-hunting proper. He thereupon acquired various neighbouring manors by exchange or confiscation. It was Wolsey who built the two walls which run in a line from the palace gardens to Kingston Bridge. Some of the enclosure was later paled or fenced, but the greater part is still in small, dark-red Tudor bricks, relieved in places by lines of even darker burnt brick forming chequered patterns and also, in at least one place, the outline of a cross, said to be emblematic of the cardinal's papal aspirations.

While Wolsey was responsible for the enclosure systems which would safeguard his hunting preserves, it was Henry VIII who stocked the parks with deer, pheasants and partridges, as well as constructing a large rabbit warren, which came to be known as the Hare Warren. Contemporary expense accounts show an item paid to 'makers of buries [burrows] for blake conies in the new warren'. These holes were bored with 'a great long nagre of irne [iron auger]'. In those days all game, including rabbits, constituted a welcome relief to everyday fare which otherwise was restricted, in winter, to tough and often partially decomposing salted beef and mutton. During Henry VIII's reign some of the land was leased, and local men were permitted to practise archery at 'certain goals' in the Home Park.

71

James I, that unattractive monarch, who was certainly no sportsman according to English standards, elected to take cover behind trees in the park and to shoot tame deer when they were happily browsing. He had little patience with the etiquette of *le sport Anglais* with which he entertained distinguished foreign visitors. Charles I's main contribution was the introduction of a new source of water, as outlined in Chapter 15.

The Manor was sold in 1651, and in that year Oliver Cromwell took up residence in the palace. But financial difficulties followed immediately, and in the next year it was decided that the parks, palace and gardens must be sold for cash. The land was divided into lots, and no embargo was put upon the demolition of the Tudor palace. However, there was a stay of sale five months later. Following further vacillation, Bushy Park was put up for sale and, together with the King's Meadows bordering the Thames, fetched £6,638 7s od, that figure including deer and timber. The purchaser promptly resold the lots at a profit, but the palace and the remainder of the Home Park were reprieved. Later, when Cromwell became increasingly powerful as Lord Protector of the Commonwealth, the lands were bought back by the State, though at a high premium. Cromwell remained in possession until his death in 1658.

After his restoration, Charles II used the palace as a hunting-lodge, particularly for the entertainment of eminent personages. At the same time he was very much concerned with improving Crown property. John Evelyn, the versatile diarist, one of whose interests was arboriculture, recorded as early as June 1662 that 'sweet lime trees' were planted on what hitherto had been flat and naked ground. He referred to the two avenues radiating from the east front of the palace, at an angle to the Long Water. At that time the lake extended the full distance from Hampton Court Palace to the Thames. Evelyn also mentions the 'perplex'd canopy' of trees known as Queen Mary's Bower in the palace gardens, though he mistakenly refers to them as hornbeam, whereas they are in fact wych elm, skilfully pleached.

In all his improvements to the Home Park, Charles II was activated by the French style of formal landscaping. His gardener, Rose, had been a pupil of Le Nôtre, that genius in the art employed by Louis XIV at Versailles. The result was that precedence was given to formal avenues, ornamental water, and a geometric layout. Charles II also set about protecting game from poachers, though at the same time he ingratiated himself with local people by reopening a public right of way through the Hare Warren which had been closed by Cromwell.

Luckily for the parks, William III abandoned a plan to resite his palace at Kempton Park. He employed Sir Christopher Wren as his designer at Hampton Court and Bushy. To Wren must be attributed the magnificent avenue of horse chestnut trees planted in 1699, whose blooms attract a multitude of visitors in the flowering period—usually early in June. In fact, though its exact date cannot be anticipated, Chestnut Sunday is prominent on the tourist calendar. Flanking the chestnuts there are four lines of limes. The avenue is a mile long, sixty feet wide, and the road has a margin of turf measuring fifty-five feet on each side before the lines of trees begin. Its length is broken to the south by a vast circle, 800 feet in diameter, in the centre of which there is a great basin, exactly half that size, which now contains the so-called Diana Fountain. Unfortunately this is cruelly out of proportion to its surroundings, having been removed from its original position in the Privy Garden of the palace.

Wren's intention had been to continue the road with its ranks of trees as far as the Great Hall of the palace, where it was to end, after crossing a bridged moat, in an enormous courtyard. But his patron, William III, died in 1702 before the scheme could be carried out, as a result of an accident in the park when the horse he was riding stumbled over a molehill and threw him to the ground. The circumstances gave rise to the well-known Jacobite toast to 'the little gentleman in black velvet'.

William III was no ardent follower of hounds. He limited his sporting activities in Hampton Court Park to coursing, and it has been suggested that he discouraged preservation of the roaming deer because of his concern for his newly planted trees. Deer and conservation are often at odds. On the other hand, Queen Anne enjoyed the pleasures of hunting. According to an eyewitness she could be seen following hounds

73

'in a chaise with one horse which she drives herself and drives furiously like Jehu'.

Bushy Park and Hampton Court Gardens were thrown open to the public after the accession of Queen Victoria in 1837, and finally the Home Park was opened in 1893. However, there had existed since time immemorial, certain rights of way through Bushy Park. These had been the cause of constant friction and even violence. The final battle was won in 1752 by the village shoemaker, who had dedicated his life to preserving a public path for pedestrians through the Hare Warren, which had been closed by the second Lord Halifax who was ranger and keeper during the reign of George II.

Much of Hampton Court Park is today taken up by its golf courses, but this does not inconvenience park visitors who, however, should keep an eye open for tee-shots, and ears pricked for a cry of 'Fore!' The imperturbable deer come off unscathed. Bushy Park is so large that riding does not have to be limited to specific tracks. Indeed, Bushy is in many respects reminiscent of a country estate. Much of the arable land grows feed for the deer of both parks, and farm animals are taken in to graze on the agister, or *per capita*, system. There are in all about a hundred acres of woodland gardens, comparable to Richmond's Isabella Plantation.

The superintendent of these two parks has to be more of a Jack-of-all-trades than most. He is responsible for the stylised palace gardens, which vary considerably according to historical period, and he also plays an agricultural role in Bushy Park. Trees, of course, must be one of his special interests. When the famous chestnuts have to be replaced, or provided with ultimate successors, varieties with a longer flowering period are being planted. One of the more newly planted lines of limes subsequently turned out to be a faithful repetition of an older, vanished avenue, dating from 1741. While the palace gardens have specialised staff, including a nurseryman known as a propagator, a Keeper of the Maze and a Keeper of the Great Vine (a woman gardener and not the holder of a sinecure), Bushy Park's complement includes a deer dresser and a gamekeeper. In all the industrial staff numbers about 160.

It has been estimated that the two parks, the palace and gardens have from 1,250,000 to 1,500,000 visitors every year. This is an approximation, because as there is no entrance fee or turnstile, the estimate relies on spot checks. However it is certain that as a tourist attraction Hampton Court Palace, with its gardens and surrounding land rate second only to the Tower of London.

8

GREENWICH PARK

In its long history, Greenwich has had to face an environmental change which fell little short of disaster. From the sixteenth to the eighteenth century, the neighbourhood was held in high repute for its clean air, and so became the resort of kings and queens, who found relief there from the pressures of metropolitan life. The greatest period of building occurred in the seventeenth century under Charles II, to be followed by the Georgian domestic architecture which is nowadays jealously safe-guarded by the Greenwich Society. But all this was to be affected by the Industrial Revolution and the growth of the Port of London, and even more disastrously, by the siting of enormous power stations at Green-wich and Deptford. Fogs and soot-laden atmosphere became the norm. Greenwich declined as a residential area, the grass was dirty to the touch, and evergreen trees and plants in the park suffered. Most indica-tive of all, the Royal Observatory which had functioned since 1675, has been forced in modern times to move to Herstmonceux in Sussex be-cause air pollution seriously interfered with astronomical observation.

Greenwich had to wait for the Clean Air Acts of the late 1960s before being reborn. Luckily, its architecture has weathered those dark ages, and the park now functions as a clean and graceful pleasure ground, used not only by the sophisticated town dwellers who have returned to live in Greenwich and Blackheath, but by the poorer occu-pants of dockland. Lunchtime finds many parties of children picnicking in the park. Unfortunately there has been a traditional pattern of hooliganism and often violence, particularly at weekends and in the late afternoons. The result is that strenuous security measures had to be adopted, and the present-day public is protected by keepers equipped with radio, dog handlers and, more recently, a mounted patrol, all of which have combined to suppress the adolescent gang warfare which previously bedevilled the precincts of the park.

Should enclosure be taken as the criterion, Greenwich is the oldest of the ten Royal Parks. However, in point of being 'royal', St James's Park is the veteran. In 1433 Humphrey, Duke of Gloucester and uncle of Henry VI, was granted by Parliament a licence to 'enclose two hundred acres of their land, pasture, wood, heath, virses and gorse thereof, to make a park in Greenwich', which had until that date formed part of Blackheath. The duke then constructed a castle on the highest point, where the old Royal Observatory now stands, and for good measure built for himself a riverside house known by the charming name of Placentia. Both these properties were taken over by the Tudors, Placentia being developed into a great royal palace in which Henry VIII and his two daughters were born and Edward VI died. The first park keeper had been appointed in 1486, one year after the accession of Henry VII.

Queen Elizabeth I favoured Greenwich Palace above all her other properties, though in her time the park was neglected, in that it was allowed to keep its original character as heathland with a few isolated oak trees, one of which, though it died in the late nineteenth century, has its stump preserved, and is known as Queen Elizabeth's Oak.

In 1619 James I replaced Duke Humphrey's palings with a brick wall. The cost was £2,000 for the two-mile length. Many sections are still in good condition, though it is difficult to identify them because the authorities have taken care whenever possible to re-use the original bricks for repairs. Otherwise, the old bricks have been painstakingly matched with new. The wall was later lowered alongside Maze Hill and Crooms Hill, on opposite sides of the park, so as to allow the fine houses there both to see and be seen.

Royalty continued to frequent Greenwich. In 1618 James I commissioned Inigo Jones to build the Queen's House for his wife, Anne of Denmark, and later, in 1635, it was completed by Charles I for Henrietta Maria. Charles II disliked the previous riverside palace and pulled it down. Though he had plans for rebuilding, these went no further than the creation of a single block which was later to be converted by Sir

Christopher Wren, under the patronage of William and Mary, into a hospital for seamen. The Queen's House, with adjacent buildings, now houses the National Maritime Museum. As far as Greenwich Park was concerned, the most important development stemmed from the interest of Charles II in science. He commissioned Wren in 1675 to build what was to become the Royal Observatory or, according to the architect, a building 'for the Observator's habitation and a little for Pompe'. In realisation, the architectural lines are too pure to be pompous. A façade of red brick with stone dressings screens the beautiful octagon of Flamsteed House, as the observatory came to be called in honour of the first Astronomer Royal, the Rev John Flamsteed. Following the removal of the Royal Observatory, lock, stock and telescope to Sussex, Flamsteed House was adapted by the National Maritime Museum to house a collection of astronomical, navigational and horological instruments. Replicas of Tompion's 'great clockes' ordered by Dr Flamsteed at a time when pendulums were a novel device, are one of the exhibits. They stand below the portrait of King Charles II in the octagonal room which was expressly designed to accommodate them. Afternoon showings are laid on in the Planetarium, the Victorian domed structure not far from Wren's main buildings.

Greenwich enjoys universal fame for its appropriation of the meridian, zero degrees of longitude, as its exact position, thus setting the standard for Greenwich Mean Time. The spot is marked by the Meridian Stone, outside the south block of the observatory. Observers like to stand astride the line, with one foot in the eastern, and the other in the western hemisphere. The gatepost is inset with the clock, set to GMT, which operates the metal ball at the top of Flamsteed House. Every day since 1833 this landmark and timepiece for mariners has dropped from its position below the weather-vane at 13.00 hours precisely.

While Sir Christopher Wren was thus busying himself creating some of the finest contemporary architecture in the world for his patron, Charles II proceeded to improve the grounds at Greenwich. It is almost certain that Le Nôtre visited England and, amongst other commissions, prepared plans for the complete reconstruction of the park. Charles II is known to have applied to Louis XIV in 1662 for the services of that grand master of landscaping, to help him 'especially at Greenwich'. Louis chose to be politic, if reluctant: 'Although I have ever need of Le Nôtre, who is fully occupied for me at Fontainebleu, I shall willingly permit him to make the journey to England since it is the King's wish.' Any doubts as to Le Nôtre's arrival in England, if not in Greenwich, seem to be dispelled by the *Hatfield Papers* which contain a warrant issued on 25 October 1662 permitting Le Nôtre to transport six horses to France customs free. Hawksmoor, in his history of Greenwich Hospital in 1727 refers to, 'The Regular Designs of that Most Admirable Person Monsieur Le Nôtre in the Esplanades, Walks, Vistas, Plantations, and lines of that beautiful park.' But this theory that Le Nôtre was the author of the grand design, can be criticised on practical issues. The spacious formal *patte d'oie* layout, so completely Le Nôtre's before he was copied by lesser men, is far from effective. The reason, quite simply, lies in the contours of Greenwich Park. Running across its centre, rising to a height of a hundred feet above the northern park boundary, there is a steep escarpment which once marked the course of the Thames. This means that no real benefit derives from the splendid pattern so well described by Hawksmoor. Any person entering from the south at Blackheath bent on using the grand processional central avenue would forge ahead to reach only thin air, at a point where General Wolfe stands against the sky staring stonily in the direction of Quebec. The abrupt fall of ground, breath-taking in its presentation of Greenwich's fine architecture, the Thames and London, completely cancels out the schematic inspiration. Can it be, as some critics suppose, that though Le Nôtre was responsible for the design of this park, he never visited the site, and assumed it to lie on level, riparian ground? Certainly, if he did visit England, Le Nôtre stayed no more than a short time and when he departed he left behind a group of French gardeners headed by Gabriel Mollet, who were judged capable of executing his various designs and maintaining the grounds upon completion. According to the diaries of John Evelyn and other sources, a grand planting scheme was initiated in 1660, to culminate in the Chestnut Avenues, and more than 1,000 elms were planted between 1663 and 1665. Sixteen coppices were formed at this time.

79

The issue of the authorship of the design is far from academic, because under the direction of the Advisory Committee on Forestry a valiant attempt is at present being made to reconstruct the park more or less according to the Le Nôtre plan. Paragraph 18 of their report dated 1964 says:

There is no doubt from direct observation that the exactly recorded design was in fact executed. The present state of the Park is due to the neglect of the 18th century, to the contrary ideas of policy in the 19th century and to the consequences of its use as a Public Park—the debasement of the design by the creation of cross paths and the slow obliteration of the ground modelling. Most old prints since 1770 indicate the decay in formality, and it may be that this gradual change is characteristic of the English temperament.

The report goes on to make recommendations as to this restoration, the most important being work on the much trodden steep slope with the object of reforming it into giant grassy terraces—Hawksmoor's 'Esplanades'—below the Wolfe statue. These may have been planned to carry a series of cascades. Hard core paths would lessen wear and tear, one of the most damaging practices being sliding and rolling or otherwise using the ground as though it were a dry-ski run. The committee also recommended the introduction of a holly hedge as a means of integrating the upper and lower landscapes.

Visitors to the park who struggle up to the halfway stage, or approach it more easily from the Blackheath Gate, will have as their reward one of the finest possible views. The panorama is even more extensive when seen from the terrace of the old observatory, because from here there come into sight not only the nearby classical architecture, the docklands and the spread of London in the distance, but also a down-river view. Another prospect, this time from the top of One Tree Hill—better wooded now—takes in Sydenham with its memory of the Crystal Palace and its days of glory in another Royal Park.

Rewarding viewpoints and interesting exhibits within a Wren building—these by no means exhaust the pleasures of this not very large

Royal Park. The Flower Garden, which shares the south-east corner of the park with the deer in the Wilderness, is as much a sanctuary for humans as it is for birds. The Ranger's Lodge is near the opposite top corner of the park, and has a good rose garden; it is now run, under licence, by the GLC as refreshment rooms. This building, with its fine Georgian proportions, was once the home of Lord Chesterfield, the statesman who wrote the classic letters of advice to his natural son, Philip Stanhope. Cricket, with a village green atmosphere, is played in the field opposite.

This story of Royal Greenwich would not be complete without a little more history. The park has ancient barrows in which stone coffins, probably dating from the Bronze Age, were discovered. And there are traces of a Roman villa which would have stood within easy reach of the road from the Kentish coast to Londinium. Nowadays, our best, if not the quickest way to the metropolis, is by river from Greenwich Pier to Tower Bridge or Westminster.

9

DESIGN

Because they originated either as royal hunting grounds or gardens attached to a palace, none of the Royal Parks, Regent's Park excepted, were designed within the context of town planning. They were primarily open spaces which came to be enclosed, first by palings, then by walls, and the majority at a later date by railings. The essential features were woodlands for cover, open space for pursuit, and grazing and watering places. Later, successive styles of landscaping were superimposed upon parks which lent themselves to the creation of pleasure gardens by famous masters of that art: Sir Christopher Wren, Decimus Burton, John Nash and possibly Le Nôtre. Behind the experts were the patrons without whom excellence could not have been achieved and who, besides acting as presiding geniuses, lived in or near the royal purlieus and enjoyed them to the full without, eventually, any prejudice to the interests of the common people. The existence of royal residences so close to each other is explained by the fact that in the early days the great seldom resided continually in any palace or mansion, the lack of adequate sanitation making it necessary to organise at least an annual Augean cleansing.

With this centuries-old legacy, there is little need for modern redesigning. Preservation, upkeep and provision for continuity are the main preoccupation of those men who are responsible for the Royal Parks. Any necessary changes tend to be gradual, the cost being absorbed by Treasury funds and the work executed by an existing labour force. The public may not be aware of the vigilance which dictates minor changes. In the case of footpaths, for instance, a watch is kept on stretches of unduly worn grass, not so much for the purpose of cordoning off the area while resowing or returfing, but with the more practical intention of creating a hardcore path wherever the need for one has been demonstrated. This means that grassy areas are spared from undue wear. Practical issues may work to aesthetic advantage. The fountains in St James's Park lake, for instance, were sanctioned in the interests of biological conservation, in that they oxygenise standing water.

The design of every park tends to change, though imperceptibly, because even a newly planted avenue will take years before it can make much impression. It is perhaps the introduction of architectural features which produce the greatest reaction from the public. The usual pattern is an initial conservative opposition, no doubt originating from the disturbance and mess inevitable during excavation and building, and before the new structure has had time to settle into its surroundings. Later may come a general acceptance which is not far removed from approval. This, for instance, may be true of Forte's Serpentine Restaurant, which is placed in such close contact with Rennie's graceful bridge. At first, Patrick Gwynne's design seemed unduly intrusive, though it can be said to fulfil an aesthetic function in providing contrasting shapes and planes in relation to a traditional scene based on horizontals. As for the same architect's café-restaurant at the lower end of the water, it no longer seems offensive, except possibly in respect of practical design, which entails badly screened loading and unloading service areas. Such architectural innovations are few, however, and have usually been made in the interests of catering, which is a vital amenity. Whenever possible, existing houses have been adapted for this purpose, as for instance Pembroke Lodge in Richmond Park, and the Ranger's Lodge in Greenwich Park.

Statues and fountains come directly under the Department of the Environment, who have accepted the policy that memorials are no longer in keeping with the character of the parks, which already contain more than enough. In fact it can be said that the existing statuary lacks distinction except, occasionally, as focal points of landscaping. Otherwise the significance of memorials seldom stands the test of time. Nor does public reaction remain constant. It is difficult to take seriously the moral indignation engendered by the naked hero in the erroneously named Achilles statue at Hyde Park Corner when it was dedicated to the Duke of Wellington by his too brazen countrywomen; or to find justification for the bedaubing with paint suffered by Epstein's inoffensive though perhaps inapposite kitcat of Rima on the W. H. Hudson memorial in the bird sanctuary at the centre of Hyde Park. But even the Peter Pan statue in Kensington Gardens has been ignominiously tarred and feathered. The second Epstein—the 'Rite of Spring' or 'Pan Group' in the shadow of the Bowater Building at Edinburgh Gate in Hyde Park—attracts little notice, so beleaguered by traffic as it is on its narrow site. Of them all, perhaps the Albert Memorial has weathered changes of taste the best, though many people regard it as little more than a monumental curiosity, or even a prolix statement of the Prince Consort's identification with the Great Exhibition.

Few of the statues are earlier than Victorian. The majority date from the between-the-wars period, a time not notable for lavish spending. However, such monuments are rarely financed from official funds; the money is raised by subscription. The earliest is the 'Diana' Fountain by Fanelli *circa* 1640 in Bushy Park, which was moved to its present position towards the end of Queen Anne's reign, and the most recent the 'Joy of Life' Fountain, erected in 1963 near the eastern boundary of Hyde Park by the Constance Fund, which came into existence in 1944 with the aim of promoting park sculpture.

Probably it is as well that monuments do not lightly come and go in the Royal Parks, otherwise there would be need for some elephant's graveyard in which the most cumbersome and outdated might have to await a resurrection day of popular taste. However removals to new sites have been sanctioned from time to time, the overwhelming force being the juggernaut of London's traffic, such as has radically altered Marble Arch and ridiculously isolated Lord Byron and his dog not far from Hyde Park Corner.

Traffic, of course, constitutes the greatest threat. The eastern boundary of Hyde Park has lost far more than the actual twenty-three acres swallowed up by the Park Lane traffic scheme, even though defensive measures in the form of mounds made of excavated material were created with the object of screening the mutilated park from the roar of encroaching traffic. The Park Lane car park to the north, being under-

Page 85   *Kensington Gardens:* (above) *View across the Long Water to the Statue of Physical Energy;* (below) *Hampton Court Palace, the Maze*

Page 86 *Entertainment:* (above) *The bandstand in Hyde Park;* (below) *Regent's Park's open air theatre*

ground, has influenced the Marble Arch corner only minimally, and cannot be blamed for the senseless marooning of Marble Arch itself in a very uncomfortable pedestrian area now surrendered to the GLC. However, in the construction of similar subterranean developments there is always a danger, difficult to predetermine, that the water-table of a large area may be affected, with damaging results to vegetation, particularly trees. But in this case the worst seems to have been averted, and except for ultra-sensitive park users who remain conscious of the catacomb-like space below them, there is little amenity interference. And one damp patch in the grass is favoured by seagulls, who add a little incident to an otherwise featureless corner of the park. Similarly the new Green Park underground station may settle in eventually. Sanction for it was given on the understanding that the surface area would be restored to pristine condition.

Another ever-present threat to the Royal Parks is visual encroachment by developments which punctuate the skyline and upset the scale of the landscape. Control does not rest wholly in the hands of those responsible for the wellbeing of the parks, because many other interests are involved. The consolation is that plans for new buildings, whether or not within range of these jealously preserved open spaces, come within the sphere of the Department of the Environment, which itself is responsible for the Royal Parks. Their influence now applies both to governmental and private building. The luckiest of London's open spaces has been Regent's Park because, after a great deal of argument and protest at the large sums of money involved, the original Nash Terraces bounding the park have retained their exterior form. And most people would agree that the Elephant House and the Mappin Terraces of the Zoo do contribute to the view from the park. The flats at Roehampton have come in for criticism as impinging upon Richmond Park, but there are two things to be said in exoneration: they are of excellent design and, also, Richmond Park is so large that the occasional peripheral development is unlikely to diminish its proportions.

The central parks tell a different story: should they be hedged about by high-rise monsters all sense of scale will be lost, in wilful destruction of the artifices of the original designers who aimed at some illusion of

F

limitless horizons. The Hilton Hotel in Park Lane was the first shock to a public conditioned to the splendid eastward view from the Serpentine Bridge. Though the hotel's plans were opposed both by the London County Council and the Royal Fine Arts Commission, the project was juggernauted through in the interests of its potential as a dollar earner. But though the Hilton still has its detractors, its inappropriateness in that particular setting has by now been largely overwhelmed by the enormity—and the word is used advisedly—of Sir Basil Spence's Horse Guards Barracks, inside the Knightbridge and Kensington Gore boundary, completed in 1970. How much better if the Crystal Palace could have been left unmolested on its original site nearby. We are told that the horses are happy in their quarters, but then they occupy the least offensive part of the complex. Someone must have overlooked Section 6 of the GLC Greater London Development Plan, which recommends 'special care for the quality of the parks and character of park-side area and skylines' and 'continuity of landscape from Kensington Gardens to Whitehall'.

Within this context, and in view of the principle that the higher the rise the greater the distance it affects, a current project is to be feared. Queen Anne's Buildings, admittedly unlovely, situated south of St James's Park, have come down, and the site is to be developed for governmental occupancy. To the time of writing, the new plans have not been published, though the sixteen-storey design has been described by Osbert Lancaster in the *Daily Express* as 'an appalling combination of an old fashioned Hollywood set for the Fall of Babylon with a cluster of provincial French water-towers'. If only half of this is true, the beauties of St James's Park will be severely curtailed. To quote Andrew Sinclair from an August 1972 issue of the *New Statesman*, where he testifies to his idea of metropolitan parks: 'Green spaces in a city need hedges, trees, hollows, meanderings, divorce from traffic and, if possible, no brutality of Basil Spence's to compete against the forest and lose the trees.' Perhaps some consolation may be derived from the knowledge that this scheme was originally promoted in the days before governmental departments were subject to the same restrictions as private developers. In future our central parks, especially St James's, which is at greatest hazard on account of its small size, may have a fairer deal, and the public given greater opportunity for registering objection.

It is an elementaty principle of park design that an illusion of space can be achieved by disguising boundaries by means of mounds and trees and that, conversely, peripheral edifices diminish the scale and reduce spatial freedom. Lilliputian schemes of tree-planting and earthworks are impotent against major 'brutality', but they can do much to counteract minor impingements. In fact, trees serve a dual purpose, in that they operate additionally as a blanket against noise. It has been calculated that every five-yards depth of trees reduces the sound of traffic by one decibel. Fountains and other running water also mute outside noise, as well as focusing the eyes upon the park itself to the exclusion of distant and probably ruder shapes. These facts were instinctively recognised by the original designers of the Royal Parks, and continue to be followed by those responsible for rearguard actions.

It may be regretted that the Royal Parks were never given the opportunity to take their place within the Abercrombie Plan of 1943–4, which never got off the ground. The proposal was that there should be twenty-four open spaces in the form of wedges, driving into central London. Within this scheme, Greenford and Wormwood Scrubs would lead to Holland Park, Kensington Gardens, Hyde Park, Green Park and St James's Park; Mill Hill to Hampstead Heath and Primrose Hill and Regent's Park; Foots Cray to Blackheath and Greenwich Park; and Richmond Park, Hampton Court and Bushy Park would drive inwards by way of Putney Hill and Barnes Common. Though the time is obviously too late for expansion, contraction must be fought, and is being fought, against an array of conflicting interests.

10

ADMINISTRATION AND MANAGEMENT

Apart from a temporary period of Parliamentary tenure following the execution of Charles I in 1649, when lands owned by the late king were temporarily appropriated and sold or scheduled for sale, the first major change in management came with the Crown Lands Act of 1829. This enacted that

> . . . all Honours, Hundreds, Castles, Lordships, Manors, Forests, Chases, Woods, Parks, Messuages, Lands, Tithes, Fisheries, Franchises, Services, Rents, and other Land Revenues, Possessions, Tenaments and Heriditaments whatsoever (Advowsons of Churches and Vicarages only excepted), which now do belong to His Majesty or hereafter shall belong to His Majesty, His Heirs or Successors within the Ordering and Survey of the Court of Exchequer in England or Wales, in Ireland, in the Isle of Man, and its Dependancies . . . hereinafter for the Sake of Distinction called the Possessions and Land Revenues of the Crown, to which the Act relates shall be under the Management of the present Commissioners of Woods, Forests and Land Revenues, and of the Successors, to be from Time to Time appointed by His Majesty, His Heirs and Successors by His or Their Letters Patent. . . .

It is significant that the document proceeded to emphasise that though the commissioners of the day were invested with powers to sell or lease other Crown Lands, in this respect, royal forests, parks or chases were excepted. The exception applied to the majority of what became the Royal Parks.

Another Crown Lands Act followed in 1851, authorising the Commissioners of Her Majesty's Public Works & Buildings to take over the duties and powers exercised by the previous authority in respect of specified Crown Lands. The list included not only the ten Royal Parks under present consideration, but some of London's other open spaces, as well as Royal Parks as far afield as the Phoenix Park in Dublin, and Holyrood Park, Edinburgh. Administrative expenses were to be met from monies voted by Parliament, while any income derived from the lands was to be paid into the Treasury. The legal position was strengthened by the Regulation of the Royal Parks & Gardens Acts of 1872 and 1926, which defined the parks and their management, as well as setting out a schedule of regulations to be observed by park users.

Nowadays the Royal Parks are run by the Department of the Environment, which inherited the responsibilities of the Ministry of Public Works & Buildings in 1970. What is known as a statutory instrument, ie a process used for subordinate legislation and requiring an interval between publication and becoming law, regularised the change. The department is headed by a Secretary of State, supported by three junior ministers and a Parliamentary Under-Secretary. These are political appointments, and change with each government. But as with other government departments, the Civil Service machinery provides continuity. Powers are channelled downwards from the Head of the Civil Service, through the Director of Ancient Monuments & Historic Buildings and other officials until a level is reached where a single civil servant heads a department exclusively concerned with the administration of the Royal Parks and various other Crown Lands in London.

This stratification inside the Department of the Environment may appear to be remote from the actual day-to-day working of the Royal Parks. To some extent this is so. These officials, permanent or otherwise, are primarily concerned with policy. They advise on issues which might affect the constitution or physical integrity of the parks, as well as upon the range of amenities and facilities which are associated with them. When these open spaces are threatened, from whatever quarter, their task is to present a case to Parliament. Legislation may then be steered through the House, or answers provided either to Parliamentary questions or by correspondence with various interested parties, or even with the individual members of the public who frequently write in with some complaint or query.

At top level, the department's role is legislative; but not all policy matters need to be debated. There are precedents and recognised principles to act as guidelines. The overall and emphatic policy is to preserve the Royal Parks as places of public recreation and relaxation which must not be encroached upon in any way which might interfere with their availability to the public at large. Except in special cases, the appropriation of any particular part of the parks for the exclusive use of a limited section of the community is forcibly resisted. Since the department has no power to assign or lease the park lands, not even to another authority, it requires a special Act of Parliament to legalise such transactions. Examples in recent times have been the creation of the Park Lane underground car park in 1962, and the dual carriageway traffic system, which lopped twenty-three acres off the total acreage of Hyde Park. Both these works were deemed to be for the public good, and were sanctioned by specific legislation.

The constitutional standing of the Royal Parks thus protects them from abuse, except after prolonged debate. And since in present times no leaseholds are granted there is no danger that any person, company or authority will be able to claim rights over land or buildings on the score of prolonged tenure. On the other hand, it has from time to time become reasonable for certain services and amenities to be turned over to private enterprise, rather than for the department to engage in practices so far removed from its competence. In cases where land and premises are involved, therefore, the solution has been to grant licences to outside operators. Catering and boating are examples.

At the same time there are always exceptional measures to meet exceptional cases, as instanced by the Royal Zoological Gardens. Regent's Park has lent itself to different treatment, in that it has a history of relatively small land divisions and leaseholds, and in fact was for only a short time maintained entire as a hunting ground or royal demesne. The Zoological Society, therefore, was allowed to lease a modest five acres at the north-eastern corner of the park in 1826, and thereafter expanded whenever possible. As recently as 1959 the Fellows clamoured for increased space but, when this was denied, the architects were forced to build high instead of wide. In point of law, within its own confines the Royal Zoological Society is independent of the parks authority, since the Royal Parks & Gardens Regulation Acts of 1872 and 1926 do not apply to the ground occupied by them. The Crown Estates Act of 1961 later confirmed the society in its right to a lease of all land occupied at that date. Similar situations, though with different outcomes, existed in other quarters of Regent's Park. The Royal Botanic Society occupied eighteen acres until it was disbanded in 1932. At that date the lease was surrendered, and the ground returned to the park proper, as is the general policy whenever a similar situation arises. St Dunstan's Institute for the Blind, most praiseworthy of institutions, was refused an extension when its lease of workshops, offices and other buildings expired in 1948. This, in point of fact, was no harsh decision; urban congestion made removal preferable. Bedford College and the two villas it also occupies are among the currently leased properties in Regent's Park. On the other hand, the well-screened area occupied by the Open Air Theatre remains under the jurisdiction of the Department of the Environment. In some cases a waiting policy is favoured, in the assurance that sectors from which the general public is at present excluded will eventually be incorporated into the park in question when favourable circumstances arise.

Where the department retains the management of certain enterprises instead of issuing licences, the reason may well be that without the imposition of high charges these could never be a paying proposition, and as such would either not attract capital investment or would discourage use by poorer sections of the community. For instance, the amenity value of the Lido in Hyde Park is so great that the department ungrudgingly bears a loss which may be heavy in sustained bad weather. Certain playing fields, golf courses and bowling greens have clubs to which members subscribe, but usually there is the proviso that basic facilities must also be available to the public.

The formulation of new policy can be of great importance. For instance, in response to criticism from some quarters in 1968 that the official line on night closing was too restrictive and outdated, the Green

93

Park stayed open at night throughout the following summer. Londoners will remember that unusually hot period, when this free dormitory space attracted persons of such various nationalities, ages, sexes and compulsions that chaos was barely averted, and sanitation problems were weightier than moral considerations. Behaviour was certainly not up to the standard of public places, let alone the Royal Parks and, with the onset of winter, the Green Park once more settled back to the old system.

An earlier experimental after-sunset opening, this time of Richmond Park in 1961, had already succeeded in condemning itself, but for different reasons: the number of deer killed by motorists escalated. Under present regulations, the park closes to traffic one half-hour before sunset, and opens at 7 am in summer and 7.30 am in winter. Its roads therefore attract a heavy load of commuter traffic. The very active Friends of Richmond Park would like the present speed limit to be reduced from 30 to 20mph. At the present time (1972) a scheme advanced by the Brentford & Chiswick Pedestrians' Association is under consideration. The suggestion is that further restrictions should be imposed upon through traffic, as distinct from vehicles carrying people to, from and around the park.

In fact, on traffic questions the Department of the Environment is bombarded by two lobbies: one consisting mainly of commuters who wish to travel with the maximum of expedition from point A to B, and incidentally to relieve traffic congestion on outside routes; the others being those local people who frequent the parks and actively oppose all threats to the environment. In traffic questions, at their most critical where Richmond Park is concerned, the department has to attempt a balance. Ever since 1934, and now perhaps nearing a climax, there has been heavy external pressure for the creation of a Petersham bypass which would involve driving a road through some as yet undefined quarter of this park. There is also a recurrent threat of a project involving the construction of a six-lane carriageway on the north boundary of Greenwich Park. This would cut off easy access to a number of attractions, including the Queen's House.

A great many issues are within the competence of the specialist

94

officers of the Department of the Environment, and some may be decided without reference to higher levels. Though the day-to-day running of the Royal Parks is not the concern of this branch of the Civil Service, the department's interest would lie, for instance, in determining the advisability or disadvantages of staging some specific event in any one of the parks. Considering the wide open spaces they provide, and the fact that they are hedged about by dense urbanisation, the central parks in particular are in constant demand. Some applications are for the permanent appropriation of ground; others for long- or short-term occupation during the staging of events, shows or entertainments. A proportion of applications are aimed at making money for the organisers; misguidedly, because this runs counter to established policy, and will incur a categorical refusal; but some are backed by charities. These too would be refused. The practice is to disallow applications wherever any charge would be imposed, or any collection taken, and this ruling cannot be circumvented by such devices as 'free' admission linked with the sale of programmes. In fact, even the free distribution of leaflets is forbidden. Some sponsored events, such as the Sheepdog Trials in Hyde Park which previously held an urban audience hypnotised, have been discontinued, it is said, because of a decline in publicity value to the promoters.

Another factor which influences the inadmissability of some project is inconvenience to the general public. The practice of cordoning off areas of the park is not favoured, and this applies even to occasions of cultural benefit. For instance, a request to produce a Shakespeare Exhibition in Hyde Park was once refused. Likewise, when Richmond Royal Horse Show's lease of the Richmond Athletic Ground expired, and a proposal was made that it should be held in Richmond Park, the application failed. If allowed to take place, either event would have created a precedent which could have proved embarrassing. An even better case for refusal was presented in 1967 against a proposal to stage a circus in Hyde Park. This took the form of the Tourist Trade Facilities Bill which was laid before Parliament by a private member, but which was 'talked out' and consequently never became law. Though on the face of it a metropolitan open-air circus appears attractive, opposition was based not only

95

on the prohibiting commercial factor, but also on the knowledge that the disturbance must disrupt the classical peace of the most central of the Royal Parks. When exceptions are made, these are likely to be for one-day events. Part of the 1972 Festival of Light came within the sphere of official tolerance in regard to Hyde Park.

Though the smooth running of large gatherings of people is the concern of the parks staff working in liaison with the organisers and the police, it is the Department of the Environment which gives the initial sanction. Sometimes, indeed, the initiative may come from its own higher ranks. For instance, in recent years a body of opinion within the department held that concessions should be made to youth by the introduction of pop concerts to Hyde Park, presumably as an antidote to conventional bandstand music. That was a time when London was still proud of its 'swinging' image. The Rolling Stones' concert in 1969 was a daring experiment, but due to the embargo on profit making, comparable concerts are difficult to arrange and the experiment seems to have lost impetus.

Though the principle of the inadmissability of charges for entertainment is regarded as absolute, it is notable that one of the most ambitious and successful events ever staged in Hyde Park was in direct contravention of this policy. The Great Exhibition of 1851 took £506,100 in gate money from 6,063,986 visitors. And though the £150,000 profit was used to purchase sites for the Albert Hall, the Natural History Department of the British Museum and the Imperial Institute, it is nowadays accepted that the enterprise was unlawful. In point of fact its legality had been unsuccessfully and expertly contested in the Parliament of the day, though in true British fashion much of the argument had centred around the threat to Hyde Park's trees. But this objection was overcome when Paxton's giant exhibition hall, the Crystal Palace, was so designed that it could contain, and even dwarf, the fullgrown trees on the site. It is pleasant to recognise that conservationists and ecologists existed long before those words were coined.

Once departmental sanction has been obtained, all arrangements and supervision of any event come within the sphere of the parks personnel. These are active, practical men who live, work, move and have their being in and around the Royal Parks. They are headed by the Bailiff of the Royal Parks, who works from an office in Westminster, but who lives in the centre of Hyde Park in a grace and favour house. Such properties are assigned by the sovereign for life or during a term of office to whomsoever she pleases. The existence of these grace and favour houses in some of the Royal Parks, and on their boundaries, are a constant reminder that the parks and their buildings remain in the ownership of the sovereign, irrespective of the fact that they are administered by a government department and operated for the benefit of the people. In early times, many of the Royal Parks were supervised by a titular ranger, assisted by one or more deputies. The position could be a sine-cure, bringing with it not only a residence in pleasant surroundings, but a salary and certain privileges. As already mentioned in connection with various parks, Ranger's Lodges, not all of which now house park officers, still exist. The appointment was in the gift of the sovereign, who usually granted it to some royal relative or nobleman, possibly in reward for his services to the nation. Many of these august holders of office identified themselves wholeheartedly with their parks, often spending a private fortune on upkeep, rather than being unduly concerned with the perquisites. However, when in the present century the administration of the Royal Parks devolved to an increased degree upon the Civil Service, the office was abolished.

Management, as distinct from administration, is represented by the Bailiff of the Royal Parks who is appointed by the usual Civil Service procedure of advertisement followed by appearance before a promotions board. It is noteworthy that the present bailiff has reached that position from the ranks or, as others might say, from the grass roots; he is a former superintendent of the Central London Royal Parks. This is a new development; previously the position had gone to eminent men, possibly without practical qualifications. The bailiff has his own office staff, and is in authority over the superintendents of individual Royal Parks and groups of parks. There are in fact five principal superintendents heading the ten Royal Parks, certain of which are grouped together for convenience, so that their resources may be pooled. Juxtaposition has created a Central Royal Parks complex consisting of Hyde Park,

97

Kensington Gardens, St James's Park and the Green Park. Because these four parks lead from one to the other, separated only by thoroughfares, they can share such things as machinery and labour, nursery gardens, etc. Their water supply comes from a common source. Other parks fall naturally into pairs: Hampton Court Home Park and Bushy Park; Regent's Park and Primrose Hill. Richmond Park and Greenwich Park, in their detached situations, each has its own superintendent.

These officers head a broadly based structure reaching down to the unskilled labourer. Absolutely every member of the staff engaged in the Royal Parks must sign the Official Secrets Act upon entering employment. This may appear ridiculous, but the explanation lies in the fact that the work involved is not restricted to the Royal Parks, but can lead to care of the gardens of Buckingham Palace and other places where security is a consideration. Hence there is no justification for derision upon hearing that the Keepers of the Maze at Hampton Court, and of the Great Vine, are put on oath not to divulge any state secrets that come their way.

So much description of the infrastructure of a bureaucracy might lead the layman to suppose that the park superintendents are typical civil servants, who might have achieved their position with only theoretical knowledge, or by recruitment from the Parks Administration Institute in Berkshire. On the contrary, they are usually gardeners or foresters, holding diplomas rather than university degrees, who have accumulated the fullest practical experience. They are able to turn their hands to many trades and professions, including simple veterinary work, and have a sound knowledge of ecology. They are public relations men, too, in that they are in constant direct contact with visitors of an inquiring disposition who come to the parks, or who find themselves in some sort of difficulty when there. It is admitted rather ruefully by those concerned that about 70 per cent of the work of a park superintendent consists of paper work. The implication is that advancement brings its penalties.

The numbers of members of staff, and the skills required, obviously vary from park to park. For instance, Richmond has its own gangs engaged upon drainage, sawing and tree lopping, supported by a paint

98

shop and blacksmiths, whereas smaller parks have to rely upon outside help for heavy work. Where required, there are gamekeepers, deer dressers and birdkeepers. As far as possible, employees occupy the gate lodges and other properties inside the parks.

Expenditure upon the 5,679 acres of Crown Lands in London—of which by far the greatest proportion consists of the Royal Parks—runs to about £2,000,000 per annum. The total cost of administering and managing the individual Royal Parks, taking the estimated outgoings and revenue for 1972–3 as guide, is seen in the following table. About half the money involved goes towards salaries, wages and materials, and in the region of £400,000 is spent on structural work in connection with buildings, walls, roads, paths, etc, and general maintenance. Over £15,000 per annum is spent on removing litter, a figure which is growing due to modern trends in packaging and the use of non-returnable bottles.

	Outgoings £	Revenue £	Net Total £
Bushy Park	86,897	4,300	82,597
Greenwich Park	223,175	2,000	221,175
Hampton Court Park and Gardens	209,135	48,000	161,135
Kensington Gardens	114,337	1,000	113,337
Regent's Park and Primrose Hill	338,810	15,000	323,810
Richmond Park	287,545	61,600	225,945
St James's, Green and Hyde Parks	595,795	61,600	534,195
	£1,855,694	£193,500	£1,662,194

Revenue is derived from various sources such as catering concessions, rents and freebords, recreational concessions, grazing, deckchair concessions, sale of timber, etc. It is immediately apparent that no attempt is made to make the parks economically viable.

11

LAW AND ORDER

Whereas in nine of the Royal Parks the law and regulations are enforced by keepers, Hyde Park comes under the Metropolitan Police, though the cost is borne by the Department of the Environment. The reason for this exception is obvious, considering that at times of political agitation crowds of up to 40,000 have converged upon Marble Arch. The present solution was arrived at in 1866, following massive disturbances. In fact, for ten years previously demonstrations and Hyde Park had been synonymous, frequently requiring emergency assistance from other authorities. The first critical mass public meeting was called on 1 July 1855, in protest against the Sunday Trading Bill. That same year, a public demonstration against the high cost of food was advertised to take place in what was referred to as 'Our Park', and though the meeting was banned, a crowd of about 150,000 assembled. The result was a bloody confrontation with police armed with staves and truncheons. Though the crowd was dispersed, the offending Bill was withdrawn the following day. This established a precedent: such Sunday morning meetings continued throughout that autumn. In May 1859 there was an orderly demonstration in sympathy with Napoleon III, but when in 1862 partisans of the Pope clashed with supporters of Garibaldi, the Irishmen espousing the former cause had to be dealt with by the military, who forced some 6,000 of them to flee in disorder 'like a herd of infuriated oxen'. They returned later to resume the conflict.

As a cumulative result of such events, a public notice was posted by Sir Richard Mayne, first Commissioner of Police of the Metropolis, on 9 October 1862. It read:

Whereas numbers of persons have been in the habit of assembling and holding meetings on Sundays in Hyde Park, and the other parks in the metropolis, for the purpose of delivering and hearing speeches, and for the public discussion of popular and exciting topics; and whereas such meetings are inconsistent with the purposes for which the parks are thrown open to, and used by the public; and the excitement occasioned by such discussion at such meetings has frequently led to tumults and disorder, so as to endanger the public peace; and on last Sunday and the Sunday before, large numbers assembled in Hyde Park for the purpose aforesaid, and, when so assembled, conducted themselves in a disorderly and riotous manner, so as to endanger the public peace; and by the use of sticks, and throwing stones and other missiles, committed many violent assaults upon persons passing quietly through the Park, and interrupted the thoroughfares; and whereas it is necessary to prevent such illegal proceedings in future: Notice is hereby given, that no such meeting, or assemblage of persons, for any of the purposes aforesaid, will be allowed, hereafter, to take place in any of the parks in the metropolis; and all well-disposed persons are hereby cautioned and requested to abstain from joining, or attending any such meetings or assemblages. And further notice is further given, that all necessary means will be adopted to prevent any such meeting, or assemblage, and effectively to preserve the public peace, and to suppress any attempt at the disturbance thereof.

The real climax came on 23 July 1866, when the commissioner's ruling was challenged by a mass public meeting in the park called by the Reform League. Unprecedented disorders resulted due, it was said by critics, mainly to provocation by the 1,700 police who had been drafted to the spot. They succeeded in closing the park gates against the protesters by 5 pm. Edmond Beales, a lawyer and one of the founders of the League, attempted to challenge the issue with the police but, in the meantime, the crowds took the matter into their own hands and, having uprooted some railings, streamed back into the park. The army was then called in but, finding that the meeting had meanwhile judiciously transferred to Trafalgar Square, they employed their surplus energy in a display of military manoeuvres. This, however, was not the end of the matter: sporadic rioting occurred on the following days. Mr Beales continued to contest the police action, basing his case upon fundamental principles which nowadays are taken for granted. His argument, addressed to Sir Richard Mayne, ran:

> The Park is either the property of the nation, as there are strong reasons for contending it is, under the transactions which have taken place between the Crown and the people, through Parliament respecting it; or it is still Crown property, though kept up and maintained out of the public purse. If the former be the fact, where is your authority for excluding the public from their property? If the latter be the case, then show me that you are acting under the express authority of the Crown, as claiming to be the exclusive owner of the Park.

Thanks to this defence, it was subsequently decided that there was nothing except the law of trespass (always difficult to invoke) to prohibit meetings in Hyde Park. Accordingly the Reform League appropriated it as their regular place of assembly, adopting as their rallying point an oak tree which stood about 350 yards west of Grosvenor Gate, but which was burnt down in 1875 by juvenile delinquents. A principle had been established, effectively putting an end to the association of the Marble Arch area with danger to the realm. This, then, was the origin of Speakers' Corner, that typically British phenomenon.

But political protest was not the only form of disorder which led to the Metropolitan Police being given responsibility for law and order in Hyde Park. Crime and vice were rampant. A letter printed in *The Times* of 30 July 1864, had described the park 'where may be seen, every day, hordes of half dressed, filthy men and women, lying about in parties and no doubt concocting midnight robberies'. Also, the park lodgekeepers were accused of neglecting their duties by opting out of all responsibility, even to the extent of refusing to open up for the benefit of hapless decent members of the public who happened to have been benighted

Page 103   *Sport*: (above) *Sailing on the Serpentine in Hyde Park;* (below) *Rotten Row, Hyde Park*

Page 104 *Wildfowl are featured in most of the park* (above) *Regent's Park;* (left) *St James's Park*

while legitimately crossing the park. In fact, a writer in the *Pall Mall Gazette* in May 1866 complained that those travellers incapable of negotiating the railings were forced to remain prisoners until the morning, amongst the most dubious company: 'A number of prostitutes, too, of the very lowest grade, ply, unmolested, in the Park, their dismal calling, spreading around them disease, until they themselves are stricken down by it, and perish in the neighbouring workhouses.' In 1866 the much needed changeover provided that 'the present system of appointing Constables for special service in the Parks under the charge of the Board of Works should be forthwith abolished and, that in future, the protection of the Parks should be confined exclusively to the Metropolitan Police Force'. Existing constables on the parks staff were then incorporated into the newly responsible police force. They retained their higher rate of pay, and 'the beneficial occupation of lodges and other emoluments'.

The actual transfer of responsibility took place on 1 April 1867, when the police assumed their new duties, including day and night patrols in Hyde Park, Kensington Gardens, St James's Park and the Green Park— in fact the four central parks. However, charge of Kensington Gardens was handed back to the Board of Works in 1887, and St James's Park and the Green Park in 1899. Though proposals to improve the police force's temporary accommodation were mooted in 1895, at a cost of £4,000, these plans were abandoned in favour of a completely new police station a short distance north of the Ranger's Lodge, for which the estimate came to £7,000–£8,000. The site and plans were approved in 1899. It seems a wry foretaste of the future that in 1903, when the final accounts were presented, the costs had escalated to £18,459 8s 7d. This capital sum, repayable over fifty years, was advanced by the Treasury, with the proviso that the building would revert to the Ministry of Public Building & Works if ever it came to be vacated by the police. The solid, unlovely but functional red-brick building at the centre of Hyde Park is a sub-station of Gerald Road police station, in SW1. It includes stables for mounted police, and not far away there are kennels for guard dogs, some of which are used for the nightly protection of Buckingham Palace. The initial policy of employing only experienced

G

police officers in Hyde Park demonstrates the degree of responsibility attached to their duties.

New Scotland Yard does not issue any breakdown of crime statistics for individual sub-stations. It may, however, be assumed that the crime rate of the parks does not differ much from the accepted general escalation in metropolitan areas. In any event, most of the offences committed are petty: loitering with intent, indecent exposure, vagrancy, soliciting and an occasional prosecution for gaming, ie operating the Three Card Trick, otherwise Spot the Lady. In fact, Hyde Park remains very much safer than, for instance, Central Park in New York City, though in the autumn of 1972 a London evening newspaper published an exposé of mugging in the central parks, claiming that this violence included vicious attacks upon down-and-outs, sometimes by setting fire to them. Figures for 1969 show that under the Vagrancy Act, in the metropolitan area, 200 men and 15 women were charged with begging, while 131 men and 24 women were charged with sleeping out —a decrease of 5 persons from the previous year. Such figures, and also brief notes on specific demonstrations, etc throughout the metropolitan area, which of course includes Hyde Park, are given in the *Annual Report of the Commissioner of Police of the Metropolis*, published by HMSO.

The staffs of the other Royal Parks are responsible for observance of the law and their own regulations, inside their own territories. The keepers are invested with powers similar to those of the police, including arrest, but invoke the assistance of the police in case of need. Soon they will all be equipped with radio. For some time mounted patrols have been used in Richmond Park—at present these are women—and now a mounted keeper has been added to Greenwich Park, which has always had special problems. The park keepers are distinguished by green flashes on their shoulders, and they make themselves of general use to the public, answering questions and sometimes directing traffic where crowds gather towards a focal point such as the Horse Guards Parade or Buckingham Palace for the Changing of the Guard. Regulations vary slightly from park to park and a relevant copy of these is posted at all entrance gates. The validity of these rules was proclaimed in the Regulation of Royal Parks & Gardens Act of 27 June 1872:

Whereas it is expedient to protect from injury the Royal Parks, Gardens and Possessions under the management of the Commissioners of Her Majesty's Works and Public Buildings . . . and to secure the public from molestation and annoyance while enjoying such parks, gardens, and possessions. . . .

The Act went on to define park keepers and their powers, privileges, immunities, duties and responsibilities as being identical with those of any police constable in the police district in which the park was situated. There followed a schedule of regulations, consisting mainly of prohibited activities. Not only did they specify the extent to which various pursuits such as riding and other sports and hobbies could be practised, but they also established a code of acceptable social behaviour. Such codes were reinforced by a further Regulation of Parks & Gardens Act of 1926.

Though couched in somewhat archaic language, for example a ban on the unauthorised 'practice of military evolutions', the regulations make sense. One aim is to preserve a peaceful atmosphere (though the prohibition against the playing of radios has become difficult to enforce since the advent of transistors), but the interests of ecology are likewise served by regulations which safeguard animal wildlife and natural growth with, where water is concerned, an emphasis on anti-pollution.

12

ENTERTAINMENT AND SPORTS

The attitude of the authorities with respect to sports and entertainments in the Royal Parks adheres to general policy. In contrast to the practice of local authorities, they subordinate such activities to wider amenities, and restrict them to definite areas. Consistent as ever, the aim is to prevent the tastes of minorities from interfering with the more general pleasures of the mass of the people. The argument is that the Royal Parks are unique, while London presents countless other opportunities for exercise. Analysis shows that it is spectator sport which is discouraged, while there is greater provision for individual recreation, such as riding and fishing. Where facilities are available for sports clubs and schools, it is a matter of principle for non-subscribing members of the public to have equal opportunity.

Culturally, Regent's Park scores with the Open Air Theatre, while Hyde Park, true to its identity as the People's Park, possesses the most popular of all recreational areas, in the form of the Lido on the south bank of the Serpentine. Hyde Park, as already mentioned, presents a special case when compared to the other Royal Parks, in that it exists for the pleasure of a vast number of users making up a complete cross-section of the public. Subsequent to its early dedication to the exclusive pleasures of the chase, it was opened to the public as recreational space much needed in a growing capital city. Foot- and horse-racing, usually in the form of matches backed by heavy wagering, were very popular. One such contest is described in *Hide Parke* by James Shirley the dramatist (1596–1666). Races between 'running footmen' were common in Pepys's day, coach-racing was reported by Evelyn during the same period, and *The Mulberry Garden*, a comedy by Sir Charles Sedley produced in 1668, gives the crowd's running commentary on a horse race. In Commonwealth times, about a decade earlier, there is a report of a hurling match consisting of two teams of Cornishmen playing fifty men a side, who 'presented great agility of body, and most neat and exquisite wrestling at every meeting of one with the other, which was ordered with such dexterity, that it was to shew more the strength, vigour and nimbleness of their bodies, than to endanger their persons. The ball they played with was silver, and designed for the party which did win the goal.' This was only one of the May Day sporting events of 1654, when from all accounts Puritanism had failed to inhibit the people, since 'much sin was committed by wicked meetings, with fiddlers, drunkenness, ribaldry and the like [enjoyed, shamefully] by powdered-haired men, and painted and spotted women'. Prize fighting promotions in the park lasted into the reign of George III. Skating was sometimes possible on the pools which became the Serpentine. Nowadays it is permitted only when the ice has reached a thickness of five inches—a rare occurrence.

But this is past history. Though May Day attracts its crowds at Speakers' Corner there are now no revels particular to the occasion. And there do not appear to be too many opportunities for wicked meetings around the bandstand, where well-tried repertoires performed by regimental bands are judged to be the most acceptable entertainment. Boating on the Serpentine has been allowed since 1847. Sailing and rowing boats are operated by a concessionaire, while safety and behavioural standards are supervised by the park's own staff. Any rowdyism is quickly quelled, yet drownings are not unknown. These can be attributed to human error, if not misdemeanour, with the lack of initiative of onlookers a deciding factor; fatalities are especially shocking in this water that rarely exceeds an adult's depth. Suicides are few, though the poet Shelley's first wife set a precedent. Rowing boats are allowed upon the Long Water in Kensington Gardens above Rennie's Serpentine Bridge. No landing is permitted on the lake shore, and the island in the Serpentine, and some of the Kensington Gardens' margin, is kept as a bird sanctuary. A special area at the extreme south-east is reserved for fishing, where grown men as well as children spend hours catching small fish which must be returned to the lake alive at the end of each day.

Though Regent's Park has sailing boats, and many of the other parks encourage bloodless fishing, only Hyde Park possesses a Lido. This open-air bathing place was the revolutionary brainchild of the socialist leader, George Lansbury, when in 1930 he was First Commissioner of Works with authority over the Royal Parks. Until that date bathing had been restricted to the early mornings, and was for men and boys only. Now-adays the Lido is run by the Department of the Environment, has a season lasting from the last Saturday in April until the last Sunday in October, and does not close until 8 pm or dusk. From 6 am to 9.30 am bathing is free, and though daytime bathing is not permitted out of season, this ban is lifted—for men only—in the early morning throughout the year. When necessary the superintendent is required to break the ice for the hardy members of the Serpentine Swimming Club. The Lido is thronged on fine summer days and a considerable space in the 350-yard-long precinct is devoted to sunbathing. The water varies in depth from two feet to seven feet six inches, at which point there are springboards, with an outer boom against encroachment by boats. Additionally, a life-saving patrol is in constant attendance, and a policeman is on duty. The water is tested by the Ministry of Health at least twice a week, and it is then decided what degree of chlorination is necessary, taking into account the temperature, number of bathers, and direction of the wind. Once upon a time the disinfection technique consisted of trailing an impregnated sack behind a rowing boat, but a piped system with per-forated arms has now been installed. The plant is situated between the Lido and Forte's Serpentine Restaurant, in line with the prevailing west wind and slight current. No adverse effect has been observed on either the animal or plant life of the lake, and it is recognised that chlorination is a necessity, in view of the fact that as many as 95,000 users have gone through the turnstiles in a peak year.

Nowadays the Lido is taken for granted as a normal amenity, but initially it attracted considerable controversy. Not every section of the public was as enthusiastic as one woman doctor, who in 1932 advocated nude bathing in what she described as a 'Nature Park'. Her suggestion was turned down by Lansbury, who said that if naked bathing were to be allowed then 'no one would be able to see the Park for the People'. The same socialist philanthropist, incidentally, was also responsible for the creation of the bowling and putting greens between Alexandra and Prince of Wales gates.

Entertainment fixtures are few in the Royal Parks' calendar. Hyde Park for instance, makes minimal provision for culture, except such as is inherent in its history; but perhaps riding and coaching have so much that is traditional in them that they have overtones beyond recreation. Created in the 1730s, Rotten Row was resurfaced with a mixture of tan and gravel towards the end of the century. Nowadays sand is used, and horsemen have the additional use of the Ladies' Mile, north of the Serpentine, and another ride running from near the Serpentine Bridge to Marble Arch, alongside the West and North Carriage Drives. Once upon a time, indeed well into the recollection of living people, riding in the Row was a social occasion, and the riders were as well groomed as their mounts. Sir Walter Gilbey, chairman of the firm of wine importers, and acknowledged arbiter in the etiquette of park equestrianism, greatly influenced behaviour and regulation wear until World War II. In fact his pronouncements upon Rotten Row manners were law. In the late nineteenth century, men wore black hunting coats, silk hats and top boots, while ladies, side-saddle of course, had regulation habits brightened perhaps by a buttonhole of violets, and silk toppers and stocks. (The vogue for bicycling in the nineties was condemned as a traffic hazard. It terrified the horses.) Nowadays things are more informal and, strangely in these days of Pony Clubs, the standard of equestrianism is vastly worse, worse even than the antics of what was known as the Liver Brigade, those Edwardian 'new rich' who rode before breakfast for health reasons rather than as to the manner born. However, the horses of the Household Cavalry stationed in Knightsbridge Barracks reproduce the colour and correctitude of bygone days.

The heyday of riders and carriages in the park continued until the outbreak of World War I but, from an insidious beginning in 1906, the changeover from horsedrawn vehicles to motor traffic had been made, and one revolution of the social whirl completed. Even so, it has not been forgotten that Hyde Park was memorable for exploits of the Whip or Coaching Club, later renamed the Four in Hand Club, members of which wore a specially designed livery and drove barouches and landaus with four horses apiece. The meets usually took place opposite the Magazine, north of the Serpentine Bridge, and the park was cleared of other traffic while the equipages careered clockwise around the park en route for Harrow on the Hill, Ranelagh or Hurlingham. These glamorous occasions are now annually commemorated by a July meet, and are becoming increasingly popular, especially since the Duke of Edinburgh has switched from polo. Other annual Hyde Park fixtures include an August London Riding Horse Parade in Rotten Row, which controverts criticisms of everyday riding standards, and the Veteran Car Run to Brighton in November, which makes an early start from the Serpentine Road. Kensington Gardens, too, has a Concours d'Elegance for Bentley drivers, lasting all day, in June.

But the most dashing of all occasions are the military ceremonies, which had their beginnings in the reviews of Elizabethan days. Spread throughout the year there are regimental parades, mounting of the guard ceremonies, and rehearsals of the trooping of the colour. One of the most moving is the Combined Cavalry Old Comrades memorial parade and service at the Cavalry Memorial not far from Hyde Park Corner, which is held on the first Sunday in May and sometimes clashes with May Day. Gun salutes are fired on 7 February, the anniversary of the queen's accession, on royal birthdays, and state visits. The Royal Horse Artillery come thundering down from Marble Arch to a point on the open ground west of Park Lane, and their split-second timing and pageantry fascinate the very small crowds who have sense enough to be, or have accidentally found themselves, in the park on the right day at the right time. There is little publicity.

Kensington Gardens is more retiring. Not much happens outside the little worlds of the model boat enthusiasts of the Round Pond and the kite fliers. And yet, surprisingly, Kensington Gardens has one point of experiment, in its own way as daring as the Lido. When the old tea house to the right of the road between the Serpentine and Alexandra Gate became redundant with the opening of the modern restaurant and cafeterias, it was at first suggested that the building should be pulled down. Instead of this, at the instigation of Mr Silkin, who was then

112

Minister of Public Building & Works, it became the Serpentine Art Gallery, sponsored by the Arts Council. People in accord with the almost archaic style of the Royal Parks, and the sedateness of Kensington Gardens, may be in for a surprise. There are no tasteful prints, no loan collections of old masters, no representational work by aspiring royal academicians; all is modern in the extreme, and sometimes overflows into out-of-door 'performances'. Currently, exhibitors are restricted to thirty-five years and under, though this age limit may be lifted when the season can be extended. At random, in 1972 the public was invited to 'an intensive colour voyage through a series of pvc tunnels and domes', an exhibition of expandable latex shapes, and 'a continuous series of actions centred round the theme of isolation and the various reactions to it', or 'boys larking with deckchairs in the gallery and wheelbarrow rides in the gardens'. All these art forms are worth sampling, and the experience is, of course, free. Nothing may be sold on the spot, but the organisers keep a price list and can put would-be purchasers in touch with the artists. Up to 1972 the exhibition has run from 1 April to mid-October in a monthly cycle: three weeks open and then one week for transformation. The reason for the limited season is that the building has no central heating. However, this is due to be installed, so that with any luck the gallery will henceforward be open for ten months of the year, beginning 1973-4.

The Green Park and St James's have not the same scope for sports, and in any event could not hope to rival their plebeian neighbour. One has too many trees, the other is too much of a garden. However, there is the usual children's playground near Birdcage Walk. The sanded rides bordering Constitution Hill and the Mall are more frequently used by the Household Cavalry than by the general public.

Besides making good use of its northern expanses for conventional sports, Regent's Park provides a golf and tennis school, as well as a running track near the edge of the Regent's Canal. But undoubtedly the most enterprising and praiseworthy venture in this park was the creation in 1932 of the Open Air Theatre. The first play to be presented was *Twelfth Night*, staged in a roped-off enclosure. Nowadays the theatre is a registered charity, and occupies space in Queen Mary's Gardens, just north of the Polygon Restaurant. It can seat 4,000 and has an enterprising wine and food bar, inspired by Clement Freud. Though takings are dependent upon the vagaries of English summers, enthusiasm is undimmed. Shakespeare has priority, and fits most admirably into the setting, but the works of other dramatists are performed from time to time, and there have been occasional presentations of opera and ballet.

Regent's Park leaves demonstrations and parades to Hyde Park, though with one exception: the Easter Monday Parade of the London Harness Horse Society—or, for short, the Van Horse Parade—in the Inner Circle. The event was first put on in 1904 and has continued ever since, with breaks during the two war periods. In 1922 there were 705 owners and horses participating, but since then numbers have declined, though it is hoped that a revival of interest in driving will correct the trend. Not only brewers' drays, costermongers' outfits and 'Steptoe' carts join in, but landaus and even gigs; not only heavy horses, manes and tails plaited and gay with ribbons, but high-stepping hackneys. Primrose Hill sets aside twenty acres on the north-west side of the hill for football and cricket, and there is a children's playground near the entrance to the Zoo opposite.

Greenwich Park is not much larger than Primrose Hill but has more than twice as much to offer. There are tennis courts south-west of the Metropolitan Water Board's reservoir, and cricket, rugby football and hockey are played in the Ranger's Field at the south-west corner of the park. Horses may be exercised before 7 am from April to September inclusive, and a little later in winter months. The park is also popular for school sports, but permission must be obtained from the superintendent, who will make the proviso that no posts or other markings shall be allowed to disfigure the ground. Evening concerts in the bandstand have become very popular. *Son et Lumière*, spot-lighted against the façade of the old Royal Observatory, is a recent introduction. Not only is the setting perfect, but Greenwich provides a wealth of historical matter for processional story-telling.

As befits its size, Richmond Park goes in for sport in a big way, though without prejudice to general users. There are as many as twenty-four football grounds, for both soccer and rugby; five cricket pitches;

two eighteen-hole golf courses though no tennis courts. In 1966, when the Petersham bypass project was resurrected, the Richmond Golf Club was one of the chief protesters. Their case rested on the ground that even if one only of their holes was engulfed by the scheme, that single deprivation would mean total reorganisation of the course.

Going from sports to individual recreation, model yachts can be sailed on Adam's Pond near Sheen Gate and Ham Dip Pond near Ham Gate, though motorised craft are banned in the interests of the deer who continue to frequent these waters. Fishing, under licence issued by the superintendent, is permitted in the unenclosed parts of the Pen Ponds, though bathing was discontinued in 1871. There is no restriction on ball games, and the park makes good kite-flying country, subject of course to height restrictions. The technology of that recreation has developed to such an extent that kites can be a danger to aircraft, especially in the vicinity of Heathrow Airport. Skating is permitted on every one of the ponds, though strict regulations are enforced as to the ice's thickness: three inches in the smaller ponds and five in the Pen Ponds, which are not only deeper but have a slight current. Walking is encouraged by the fact that the car parks, with one exception, are on the motor roads which circle the inside of the park. Their sites have been selected with care, so that the principal features of the park, and the open ground, should be within reach of all comers. The exception is the car park east of the Pen Ponds which, since they are almost central, might otherwise be beyond the range of short-distance walkers.

Richmond Park is excellent for riding, with its open land, safe tracks and opportunities for the observation of wildlife. Not only do the riders' extra few feet above ground level give a different and wider viewpoint, but wild animals and birds take less notice of people on horseback than when approached on foot. Restrictions are few and sensible: for a great part of every weekday riding is permitted all over the park except where it is enclosed or where there is mown grass, or on footpaths. Occasionally, on account of bad weather conditions which would involve poaching of the ground, warning notices are posted at the gates. After 1 pm on weekdays, or 11 am on Saturdays, Sundays and Bank Holidays, riders must keep to the well-defined riding tracks, or to a special riding ring.

A very small percentage of visitors go to Hampton Court, or even to Bushy Park just for sport or entertainment as distinct from sightseeing. It follows that these two parks are principally used for recreation by local people. The Home Park remains much as it has always been, and its golf course fits into it without disturbance of the environment, as do the model sailing boats on the Rick Pond. Fishing licences are issued for the Longford River and the ponds, and there is boating on the Heron Pond, football grounds near Teddington Gate, as well as a cricket pitch between Leg of Mutton Pond and Kingston Bridge. But as with Richmond, perhaps the greatest enjoyment of all is experienced by riders, who are allowed great liberty. They are not confined to prescribed tracks, but may ride over the open ground or, constrained by its perfect formality, along the wide verges of the Chestnut Avenue.

13

GARDENS AND GARDENING

The element of waste in park horticulture may shock plant lovers, though it is unavoidable when the aim is a constant display of colour. Bulbs and bedding plants must be expendable as soon as their successors are on the point of bloom. There was a time when throw-outs from Hyde Park were given to the poor of adjacent boroughs, but these days the bulk is so great, and sorting and distribution would be so costly, that the practice has been discontinued. They must, therefore, be burnt or put on the compost heap, though an exception is sometimes made for prisons and institutions. It must be accepted that the plants will have been treated roughly from the moment of lifting, and that the foliage of the bulbs will have had no chance to die down naturally. Also, the varieties have to be shovelled up unsorted. This applies of course only to bulbs from flowerbeds; those in grass, where for instance they make a heartening show on the slopes facing Knightsbridge and Park Lane, are left undisturbed even when the grass around them must be mown. Credit must be given to the late superintendent of the Central Royal Parks, now promoted to bailiff, who was inspired to set out the daffodils and narcissi by broadcasting them haphazardly then planting them where they fell, in satisfyingly irregular patterns following the ground contours.

The practice of mass destruction applies chiefly to bedding plants, though in the past perennials had similar treatment, especially those with shiny foliage and which were therefore incapable of tolerating London's polluted air. Such plants as edelweiss and gentians accustomed to rarefied atmospheres nowadays enjoy a reprieve; due to cleaner air they can remain undisturbed for a full life span. The same improved atmospheric conditions have led to the establishment of azaleas, heaths and rhododendrons in the Flower Walk in Kensington Gardens. On the other side of the ecological balance sheet, bees and butterflies are now-adays decidedly scarcer. Due to the destructive element in park horti-culture, cross-pollination is no longer of great importance.

Except for the central parks, and those which are paired, each one is independent of the others from a horticultural standpoint. They have their own glasshouses, and often tree-nurseries, with specialist super-visors and foremen, and carry on irrespective of each other, though not without some rivalry. The nursery precincts are usually well screened, for the sake of privacy as much as shelter. How many Sunday strollers in Hyde Park are aware that at its centre, not far from the Ranger's Lodge, there are four acres of glass? This hidden enclave is in process of modernisation, in an eight-year plan based on phasing out and replacing glasshouses, some of which were put up as far back as 1909. These particular nurseries fulfil a function which extends beyond the boundaries of the four central parks. They provide window-box material for government offices in Whitehall and elsewhere, and flowers for display on special occasions, such as state visits, when the Mall receives a great deal of attention. Their output, therefore, has to be programmed to the state calendar. The Queen Victoria Memorial outside Buckingham Palace is another special responsibility. The parterres here require 40,000 tulips and 14,000 geraniums annually, the imperative colour being scarlet, though subordinate shades may be included to ring a change. In all, the central parks buy in, under contract, about 500,000 bulbs every year. Their bedding and herbaceous plants, however, are raised from seed or cuttings in the nurseries, in which the late Queen Mary took great interest.

Though in policy matters each superintendent is subject to the over-riding authority of the Department of the Environment, he is very much his own master where practicalities such as gardening are concerned. Strictly, any change in design or layout—especially if it would incur abnormal expenditure—should be committed to paper and submitted through the bailiff to the higher authority. But it is not unknown for an individual superintendent to get a pet scheme going by working away at it and employing his regular labour force until the project is realised, as

118

though by magic. These superintendents are men of ideas, who at the same time can be trusted not to ride roughshod over traditions. However, there is always room for inspiration. At Hampton Court, for instance, where the layout of the immemorial gardens could not be bettered, the superintendent achieves variety within the established patterns, his intention being to provide colour in the flowerbeds from January until the end of November at least. Accordingly, the famous herbaceous border is no longer true to its description: it has annuals and even bulbs and corms planted amongst the perennials. This ensures that the flowering season will extend from the aconite to the Michaelmas daisy. Not even purists could object. Again at Hampton Court, where the delightful enclosed gardens are small, their flowers may be varied from year to year as regards colour and kind, whereas their height is dictated by the dimensions of the layout itself.

Apart from their flowerbeds, which in the case of Hyde Park were introduced in 1860, and which usually accompany paths, many of the Royal Parks boast some very special gardens. A few of these have been maintained over a long period, perhaps having started life as the formal pleasure gardens attached to a palace; others have been created in a woodland setting as a contrast to open parkland. Queen Mary's Gardens in Regent's Park have a unique history, as they evolved from the grounds of the now disbanded Royal Botanic Society. Though this society was not founded until 1838, the need for such an institution, with gardens freely available to interested parties, was mooted in 1812, at a date before Kew Gardens were opened to the public. The society was granted a royal charter the following year. The principle of taking over part of Regent's Park for horticultural use and display had been approved by John Nash, and when the lease of eighteen acres previously held by a nurseryman was transferred to the society, the grounds were laid out by Nash's pupil, Decimus Burton, in co-operation with Richard Marnock, who had been curator of the Botanic Gardens in Sheffield. The plan was ambitious but functional, consisting of various specialised areas, including a rose garden, but in the end it was the conservatory and the use of large tents for exhibitions which saved the society from ruin by offsetting the initial cost of £12,000. However, though this period of economic viability lasted nearly a hundred years, on the expiration of their lease the society was faced by such a prohibitive increase of rent that it had to be disbanded in 1932. When the area was returned to the custody of the Ministry of Works, Queen Mary took such interest in the redevelopment that the gardens were renamed out of compliment to her.

Ever since that time, the circular gardens have been beautifully maintained, their chief fame being the Rose Garden, which now contains more than 50,000 bushes, and is rated as the finest collection in western Europe. It is out-rivalled only by the Valley of Roses in Bulgaria. Fortuitously, the heavy clay of Regent's Park, which had made it unsuitable for building, could not be bettered for the purpose. From the first, the rose garden was assisted by gifts from the British Rose Growers' Association, and that co-operation continues. The superintendent of the park is also privileged to select new varieties from the rose trial grounds of the Royal National Rose Society at Bone Hill, near St Albans, previous to their reaching the market.

The present policy is to develop Queen Mary's Gardens into an all-the-year-round spectacle, rather than have its flowering season beginning with tulips in early May and ending in October. The attractions include colourful borders, a well-planted mound made from waste material from the main lake, and a most attractive small piece of water with an island rock garden patterned with alpine plants, giving a rustic Japanese effect.

Regent's Park has another, smaller and separate garden, once the private grounds of St John's Lodge, which is now occupied by Bedford College. These formal gardens, which have a single entrance leading first to a long rectangle, then a circle, then an ellipse and finally a much smaller circle, make a comparatively unknown retreat from the world. In fact anyone who writes about them does so with some hesitancy, for fear that their peace may be disturbed.

The gardens of Hampton Court Palace are world famous. Whole books have been written about them and there is not enough space here for more than a bare catalogue: the huge, colourful Broad Walk; the Privy Garden opened to the public by Queen Victoria in 1894; the Orchard Garden reserved for residents of the grace and favour apartments in the palace; the Pond Garden believed to be pre-Tudor; the Tilt Yard Garden scented by old-fashioned roses; the Wilderness near the Maze; the Maze itself, now almost entirely of yew, being more dense and durable than the hornbeam with which it was previously interplanted; and the Great Vine, planted in 1768 and still going strong, due to its being protected by glass from infection from the people who crowd inside to marvel at its tremendous dimensions. One of the most fascinating special gardens is the Knot Garden, a reconstruction of an Elizabethan horticultural conceit, which Shakespeare alluded to as 'thy curious Knotted Garden'. Its small beds are formed by intertwining ribands of clipped evergreens of different shades—box, lavender, camomile—and the flowers are stiff low-growing begonias, heliotrope, lobelia and similar plants selected for their pure colour.

Kensington Gardens, too, has its palace gardens. These are very small and secluded. They are contained by the tunnel of pleached lime trees into which squints have been cut so that outsiders may look in. Three leaden tanks culminate in a formal lilypond, there are gently graduated terraces containing well ordered perennials, and charming stonework.

Neither Greenwich Park nor Richmond has a surviving palace, and hence there are no formal gardens. Greenwich makes up this deficiency by cutting off the south-eastern corner of the park to take in the thirteen-acre Wilderness where the deer live. The flower garden there resembles that of a comfortable country house. It is attractively laid out, with huge circular flowerbeds and a small lake and islet overhung with willows. Another delightful feature is the herbaceous border on the north boundary, which has the distinction of extending for 400 yards, exceeding its rival at Hampton Court in length.

There remain those two Royal Parks whose virtue lies in open spaces where any imposed pattern of gardens would be inappropriate. In both parks it was not only their nature, but the presence of the destructive deer, which ruled out flowers except in strongly fenced areas. Richmond Park's Pembroke Lodge, now given over to refreshments, has masses of flowers, but the most exciting introduction has been the shaping of the delightful woodland garden which takes in about one third of the Isabella Plantation. This wild garden was the creation of

H

Mr George Thomson, the superintendent of Richmond Park who retired in 1971. Up to the time of his appointment in 1951, though the plantation was as interesting from a forestry point of view as the others in the park, it was no more and no less than that. But he proceeded to transform it into a garden, hidden among tall well established trees, watered by a little artificial stream falling in delightful cascades made by tiny dams of timber, with frequent crossing places, and planted with heaths, spiraea, primulas, foxgloves, water forget-me-nots and other plants which will flourish without obvious attention. There are two ponds, one named after Mr Thomson, where lilies, irises and weeping willows grow. In season the whole woodland garden, canopied by tall beeches the earliest of which were planted in 1831, is ablaze with azaleas and rhododendrons, as well as with trees and shrubs, such as Japanese maples, which have been selected for their brilliant foliage. Inescapably, the Isabella Woodland Garden has been extolled as the perfect setting for a performance of *A Midsummer Night's Dream*.

Bushy Park, which has many points of similarity with Richmond Park, is not to be outdone in the matter of a woodland garden. The Waterhouse Plantation is the creation of the present superintendent. In comparison with the Isabella Plantation, he had the advantage of an existing water supply, because the Longford River runs through the plantation. However, the comparative flatness of the ground presented more of a challenge. The area is large, and can be extended. There are lawns, and flowerbeds leading towards winding forest walks, far from the sound of human activity, but always with running water nearby. And if the feeling of peace had to be given a rating, it would be difficult to choose between these two new woodland gardens which are so well contained by trees that not only do they fail to detract from the untamed character of both parks, but can be discovered only by people who seek them out.

Those are examples of the successful introduction of cultivation into natural spaces. The central parks have to grapple with an entirely opposite problem—how to retain something of wildness in ground which is walked over, day after day, by crowds of people. A brave attempt was begun in 1972 to conserve a small area of Kensington

Gardens, off Buck Hill Walk, where the commonest of growths such as gorse, cow parsley and campion are encouraged to fend for themselves. Such a fancy for weeds might seem odd to a visiting countryman, yet it makes sense in parks where the grass is regularly mown, so that nothing has a chance to seed, and where even the native grasses have often to be replaced with harder-wearing varieties. It is nearly 400 years since Gerard recorded in his *Herball or Generall Historie of Plantes* that small bugloss or oxtongue was to be found in 'the drie ditch banks about Pikadilla'.

14

TREES

Individual and free-standing trees possessing historical or storied associations are to be found in all the Royal Parks. Equally each park usually features some plantation or avenue of a species which has been found to thrive in that particular location; soil, drainage and aspect being the prime factors which combine to promote the strong growth which results in beauty and longevity. Bushy Park's central avenue of horse chestnuts, supported by lines of limes, which extends for nearly a mile from Hampton Court Gate to Teddington Lodge is the most famous. A few of the trees from the original planting in the reign of William III still survive, though their numbers are being rapidly depleted by storm damage and old age. Greenwich Park is known to tree lovers for its avenue of Spanish chestnuts, and others of a great age are to be found in the flower garden, as are cedars of Lebanon and deodars. At least one of the Spanish chestnuts is a survivor of those brought from Lesneys Abbey in Kent in 1664 and has a girth of almost twenty-five feet. The main attraction of these venerable trees lies in their massive boles and the spiral corrugations of their bark. Richmond Park's well regulated plantations and spinneys are counter-balanced by a scattering of ancient pollarded oaks.

Hyde Park has a great many plane trees, introduced in the late seventeenth century by reason of the annual bark-shedding which made them ideal for survival in a smoke-laden atmosphere. But nowadays, following the designation of central London as a smokeless zone, there is less need for discrimination; the result is that even conifers, those trees which are least capable of ridding themselves of clogging and poisonous deposits, are now thriving in nearby Kensington Gardens. Meteorological records show that central London's December sunshine has increased by 70 per cent and smoke deposits have decreased by 60 per cent since the operation of the Act. For the same reason, the cedars and deodars of Greenwich Park, for a long time at risk, are now in better health. Planes continue to flourish in the Green Park, and weeping willows give an oriental effect to the ornamental waters of St James's. Regent's Park goes in for all kinds of indigenous trees, as well as those such as sycamore and chestnut which have become so well acclimatised as to be nowadays generally accepted as British. Some specimen exotica are justified, the reason being that this park's atmosphere is largely that of a garden, rather than a demesne or a chase, and ornamental trees contribute to this impression.

Arboriculture as practised in parks and gardens is distinct from forestry, which for the most part is directed towards the production of successive crops of timber for commercial use. The Royal Parks as far as possible aspire to uninterrupted succession. Though new plantations and even avenues are sometimes created, the main object is two-fold: preservation of satisfying lines and groupings of trees and provision for the future—in fact the maintenance of a balance between conservation and continuity of growth. The elimination of intrusive species which may have been planted as rapid-growing stop-gaps is an important secondary consideration.

Every tree has a normal span of life which may be extended by good management, much in the same way as medicine and surgery prolong human life. But ageing is inexorable, and the arboriculturalist must anticipate casualties. This is done, in parks, by the early planting of a similar type of tree adjacent to the obsolescent one. Not much use is made of newly planted semi-mature trees—say of forty-five feet or more in height—though this proven technique has recently come to the fore with the advent of a giant machine perfected by the National Coal Board. It can lift a halfgrown tree, complete with ball of roots and soil, so that it suffers minimum disturbance. For ideal results, the tree must be root-pruned in a circle the preceding year. Nothing is entirely new; similar techniques were known to the Romans, as well as having been practised by some of our greatest early landscape gardeners. In 1703 Henry Wise, William III's gardener at Hampton Court, successfully transplanted 403 lime trees of an estimated girth of from $3\frac{1}{2}$ to 4 feet. However the process is costly, even with the employment of modern technology, in fact of the order of £100 per tree, and foresight can forestall such drastic measures. The current practice is to select well-grown trees of about 8 to 10 feet. These are easier to protect than smaller ones which, however, some experts prefer on the score of rate of growth and ultimate health.

In spite of the expense which would have been incurred there might have been a case for planting semi-mature trees on either side of the Broad Walk in Kensington Gardens. Until 1953 this had been renowned for its avenue, preponderantly of elms, some of which remained from the original planting by Queen Caroline. The reason for their removal was death and decay due to old age, rather than Dutch elm disease, which is currently a nationwide threat to the species. Since gaps in avenues are not acceptable in formal park management, the trees were removed wholesale. This act caused violent controversy, weighted with emotiveness, from people unaware that as early as 1870 the superintendent of the central Royal Parks had reported on the dangerous and deplorable state of the trees, which had in fact been planted too close together in the early eighteenth century, and which had never subsequently been thinned except by act of God. In this instance, regrettably, there were no ready-sited successors, and though the avenue was immediately replanted, first with beech, many of which failed, then in 1955 with sycamores and Norway maples, and in 1958 with outer lines of limes, it will still be many years before the former grandeur of the Broad Walk is restored. And there are no elms, that very English tree.

The problems of management of park trees are immense. Not the least of these emanates from criticism from an insufficiently informed public which always has a reserve of sentiment ready to be directed against the woodman and his axe. But trees in public places must be sacrificed when they constitute a hazard. It is perhaps less easy to accept that healthy trees have to be felled to create overhead growing space for their neighbours. These replacement procedures must be adopted in woodlands where the trees are of one kind, and coeval. Nowadays, therefore, mixed plantations are favoured and, where possible, the succession is ensured by interspersing existing mature trees with others at various stages of development.

Elms have been much in the news because of Dutch elm disease. In point of fact, the disease was first recognised in London in 1927, though it did not assume critical proportions until recently. Emergency powers were at first given to local authorities enabling them to serve the owners of affected trees with a notice to destroy them or any affected part of them. Then, in late 1972, this directive was withdrawn, the reason given being that the disease had far outstripped human resources. In fact, there has always been a body of opinion which regards such drastic measures as unnecessary, in that the disease can potentially be cured or at least arrested by natural means, such as a very hard winter. Initially, the Royal Parks acted upon advice given by the Forestry Commission, which entailed felling perhaps 70 per cent of the badly infected trees. They are now settling down to what has always been general policy for all types of trees under their aegis: if any tree is as much as 50 per cent affected, and therefore dangerous or unsightly, then it has to go. Meanwhile, research has produced a fungicide which may be injected into an affected tree. This treatment must be given during the very early stages of the disease, and the cost is of the order of at least £5 a tree but, where appropriate, this remedial treatment is now given. All the Royal Parks were affected, some more than others. The greatest loss was sustained by Hampton Court's Home Park, where more than 200 elms in the Barge Walk had to be felled.

Perhaps if the general public had understood the disease more thoroughly, they might have accepted the high percentage of felling which was then thought unavoidable. The disease is caused by a fungus, which is spread by two kinds of beetle, and which becomes apparent from June onwards, at which stage the leaves of affected branches turn yellow or brown, and growing points droop. Further examination by cutting across the grain of a bough will show that the wood is ringed with dark spots. The spread of the disease is rapid: leaves fall, branches wilt and at worst entire trees may die after only a few weeks. The dead material, particularly the bark, then forms the breeding ground for the beetles, which lay their eggs in it, and from which the larvae emerge in

127

thousands in the spring. The autumn months are therefore the season for felling badly affected trees. All the bark down to ground level should be burned, though the stripped trunk may be removed for use or sale. Perhaps visitors to the central parks during 1972 will have noticed the sinister identification by blobs of paint which indicated that certain trees were due to be dealt with in this manner. The planting of elms has not been discontinued as a result of the emergency. Young trees, with their comparatively tender bark, are not so prone to harbour the beetle. Also there are two Dutch varieties of elm which are credited with greater resistance to the disease than our native product.

Though casualties among trees, whether from storm damage, disease or age, tend to attract public attention, to a certain extent the replanting of the parks continues unnoticed. This work is carried out according to the recommendations of the Advisory Committee on Forestry, which issues reports published by the Stationery Office from time to time. The committee formulated a set of principles in respect of Kensington Gardens, all of which apply to the other Royal Parks:

1 To maintain dignity and amenity.
2 To establish by appropriate stages a properly distributed succession of age classes, to ensure continuity.
3 To plant only appropriate species.
4 To protect and tend the growing trees and shrubs, and to attend to pruning and lopping.
5 To minimise risks to the public from unsound trees.
6 To main a territorial balance between plantations and open spaces.

The first official report was issued in 1954, since when a great deal of imaginative work has been carried out. Apart from the general principles, various other recommendations catch the eye: in the opinion of the committee chestnuts and limes existed in adequate numbers in most of the parks, and they favoured truly native species such as oak, ash, hornbeam (which they considered to be neglected) and beech. The planting of food-bearing trees for birds was also advocated as part of any new scheme. Berried trees such as hawthorns, hollies, pyrus and prunus were selected for food, rather than ornamental, value. They cited types of trees which might encourage beneficial insectivorous birds, and also those which would provide nesting places for hole-nesting species. The committee also reached the conclusion that the outer parks in particular should be 'so managed as to maintain the tradition of the English park landscape and the ordinary English countryside' and that native English trees (not excluding the elm on the score of its disadvantages the worst of which, at that time, was its habit of shedding limbs or falling without warning) should be given preference over foreign importations. And they underlined that long-term policies must be adopted, in order to avoid crises similar to that which caused the Kensington Gardens Broad Walk tragedy. They also deplored, perhaps too positively, the introduction of exotic specimen trees.

Tree-lovers will discover particular interest and satisfaction in the example of Richmond Park, where in the twenty years between 1947 and 1967, as many as 72,492 trees were planted, and the failure rate is as low as 5 per cent. These new trees include the pedunculate oak, which likes a boggy terrain, and which in the past was valued for ships' timbers, and the sessile oak, which thrives on better drained ground. Chestnuts, willows, hornbeams and alders have been planted, and there is no objection to foreign introductions to specific areas which these trees suit, for example the cedars of Petersham Park, which was added to Richmond in 1843 and the flowering shrubs and many-coloured maples of the Isabella Plantation. The open spaces of the park are memorable by their already mentioned great free-standing 'stag-headed' or pollarded oaks which are unique to the point of oddity, and the plantations are examples not only of good forestry but of imaginative design continued from 1813 until present times. The majority of the woodlands are fenced, not so much against man as deer, which have an even worse record as predators. Also great accent is put upon the conservation of the plantations as bird sanctuaries, for which natural undergrowth is most valuable as well as assisting in the conservation of water for root growth of the principal trees. Thus otherwise undistinguished self-sown trees may be allowed to grow as undercover, and can be removed when they have served their purpose.

The various reports of the advisory committee are well worth studying, as giving insight into the special needs of each Royal Park, and the reasoning behind changes and improvements. At present, however, they are out of print, though they may be found in libraries. Invariably, official records show that more trees are planted each year than the number felled.

15

WATERS

True to the independent character of the Royal Parks, up till now the majority have relied upon natural resources for the supply of water to their lakes and ponds. This is of special interest in the case of the truly metropolitan parks, which historically were well- and sometimes over-watered by streams flowing in from the north. Most urban dwellers take for granted the complicated network of services which exists like a dis-organised spider's web beneath their city: gas mains, electricity cables, conduits, sewers and underground railway systems. The most romantic of all these must be 'London's lost rivers'—those streams which even-tually deteriorated into foetid open drains and had to be channelled underground. Where the water was needed in the parks, if only for show, it was then introduced from a purer source. The Tyburn is one of the best known of London's small rivers, because of its nominal associa-tion with the ancient gallows near Marble Arch. But these days its subterranean existence passes unremarked, even when London's street names should recall it.

The little river which gave its name to St Marylebone—otherwise St Mary by the Bourne—church, was used in 1552 when trenches were dug 'for the conveyinge the water into two ponds which yf it hadd not ben don wode have byn the dethe of many dere'. These bricklined ponds were probably on the site of the present-day Regent's Park lake. It is known that John Nash used Tyburn water for his lake when a scheme to supply it from the Regent's Canal failed. The outlet from the lake was through a brick culvert into the new King's Scholars' Pond sewer, but the scheme revealed flaws when in the summer of 1831 residents com-plained of the stench of stagnant water. The privately owned West Middlesex Water Company then contracted to supply 23,000 tons

131

annually for £200. Another change to the lake came about as a result of a fatal skating accident in January 1867, when some 150 people fell through the ice. This led immediately to the level of the lake being lowered by filling the bottom with hard core and rubble. The average depth now is four feet six inches, without taking into account craters made by bombs in World War II. A ban on skating was imposed after the tragedy, the opinion being that the current and the existence of six islands made the ice unreliable even in hard winters. The shallowness of the lake lessened the necessary intake of water and these days it is dependent upon seepage. In times of drought the water occasionally smells unpleasant, and there is a likelihood that before long a mains supply will be brought in from a point near York Bridge. The problem has been aggravated by the wiring off of part of the lake to make a waterfowl sanctuary. Dirt, rotting leaves, feathers and nesting material collect in this backwater. It is likely that the barrier will soon be removed, even though this must create some difficulty as regards the segregation of warring geese and swans.

In the thirteenth century the Cowford Pool, in what was to become St James's Park, became choked with weeds and the adjoining land deteriorated into swamp. During the reign of James I, water was brought from Hyde Park by channels controlled by a sluice. When Charles II made his long water known as the Canal, the natural springs on the spot proved inadequate, so that an underground channel to the Thames was excavated with the object of admitting tidal water. The controlling sluice survived until about 1825. Rosamond's Pond was also connected to the Canal by a sluice.

Modern times have seen a great reversal; the water from the springs under Duck Island produces a more than adequate supply not only for St James's Park lake but also for the Buckingham Palace gardens, the Serpentine and the Long Water, to all of which it is pumped in what seems an illogical direction. The first of several interconnecting wells was sunk in 1846, the deepest being thirty-one feet. The electric pumping-station draws the water up into a reservoir for distribution, the surplus being discharged into the lake. It is surprising to discover a hidden (and barred from the public) modern power house in such a place. The engineer in charge has log books dating back to 1907, recording the levels of water and duration of pumping for each day of those sixty-five and more years. The lake in St James's Park holds about 8,500,000 gallons of water. It has a concrete bottom, and a depth of only about three feet nine inches. The Serpentine and the Long Water in Kensington Gardens, on the other hand, together hold an estimated 80,000,000 gallons. The greatest depth is below the Serpentine Bridge.

Originally the Manor of Hyde or Eia, which was to become Hyde Park, was watered by the West Bourne River, which entered from the north, where it has given its name to Westbourne Terrace. This is another lost river, the 'west' of its name distinguishing it from the easterly Tyburn. The river ran south-south-west into Hyde Park, then dispersed into eleven pools surrounded by marshland, through which another stream came in from Marble Arch direction. When it seeped out of the low-lying ground at a point near the eastern end of the Serpentine, the river ran south under Knightsbridge, and then meandered through market gardens subject to flooding before reaching an outfall into the Thames in the grounds of Chelsea Royal Hospital, where some of its water was diverted into a reservoir owned by Chelsea Waterworks. The latter stages of its course were not completely filled over until 1856–7. There is now no superficial evidence of the river's existence, apart from the enormous cast-iron pipe, part of the Ranelagh sewer, which carries the outfall from the Serpentine over the platforms of Sloane Square underground station. The pipe withstood enemy bombing when the station was almost completely wrecked in World War II. The river itself, after having been condemned in 1869 as foul, was diverted into the main sewage system at a point near the Bayswater Road. At that time fifteen feet depth of stinking mud had to be removed from the bottom of both the Long Water and the Serpentine.

To go back in history: traditionally most of Westminster, including Rosamond's Pond in St James's Park and the Chelsea Waterworks reservoir in the Green Park—both now vanished—drew water from Hyde Park. This preference for the West Bourne over the Tyburn is traceable over a long period, the reason probably being greater purity. Westminster Abbey itself took its water from a spring and conduit house in

Hyde Park until the supply failed in 1861 as a result of drainage works. The source is commemorated by an urn on a pedestal at the lower end of the Serpentine. The inscription reads:

A supply of water by conduit from this spot was granted to the Abbey of Westminster with the Manor of Hyde by King Edward the Confessor. The manor was resumed by the Crown in 1536 but the springs as a head were preserved to the Abbey by the charter of Queen Elizabeth in 1560.

However, this and a similar concession were withdrawn in 1620, when James I complained that his deer were going short of water.

In 1730, to the order of Queen Caroline, Hyde Park's pools were drained and the West Bourne dammed for the creation of the forty-acre Serpentine. Much of the beauty and amenity value of Hyde Park stems from this expensive piece of landscaping. At the same date one of the smaller ponds to the east was emptied, and became the Dell, which is now a small wildlife sanctuary. The principal works were completed in 1733, though major repairs had to be done after the lake broke its banks in 1737, causing a substantial amount of flood damage to Knightsbridge and Brompton. The normal outlet was under a footbridge not far from Albert Gate, where subterranean channels may be inspected (though not by the public) through heavily disguised masonry which is said to be the last relic of Elizabethan architecture in the park.

Hampton Court and Bushy parks owe their supply of water in their lakes and ponds to royal inspiration. This time the scheme was one of major engineering, and led not only to the convenient watering of live-stock and game, but also to the formation of the Long Water, which is such an indispensable feature of the view from the east front of the palace.

Cardinal Wolsey originally brought in water from a source at Coombe Hill, three miles away, but this supply proved totally inadequate for all except household use. The line of leaden pipes ran through the northern part of the Home Park, and is known to have functioned until 1876. Since neither park had natural water other than unreliable ponds dependent upon rainfall, Charles I looked further afield after he had been prevented by Parliament from linking his royal preserves with those of Richmond. His scheme entailed the construction of an eleven-mile channel to conduct water from the River Colne across Hounslow Heath. The plans were approved by a commission in 1638, and the work was begun in the autumn of that year and finished in July 1639. The artificial river, on average twenty-one feet wide and two feet deep, was to water Hampton Court Palace and its gardens, ponds and fountains, and also to provide drinking pools for the deer. The briefing to supply water 'for the better accommodation of the Palace, and the recreation and disport of His Majesty' succeeded, but due to the haste shown in both planning and executing what was for those times a considerable feat of engineering, critical faults soon emerged. The banks were not high enough to prevent seasonal flooding, and a great deal of indignation was expressed by local people, whose pedestrian rights of way were not only made uncomfortable, but were obstructed by rises in the level of the water. In fact, in 1648 during the Civil War, local objectors succeeded in damming the river at Longford, near its source, though it was later reopened by Oliver Cromwell, at which time he also constructed the Leg of Mutton and Heron (debased form of Hare Warren) ponds.

Nowadays the Longford River, more picturesquely known as the King's River, fills a reservoir in the Waterhouse Plantation, where its flow has been used to advantage in the creation of the woodland gardens. After that, in what gives the illusion of following a natural course, the river supplies the basin of the Diana Fountain and Cromwell's ponds in the Hare Warren—all in Bushy Park. A bifurcation goes to Syon House, the seat of the Duke of Northumberland. The water also passes through a culvert below the road separating the two Royal Parks, to feed Hampton Court's elliptical Canal and the Long Water before its overflow is directed through a sluice into the Thames. Nowadays the fountains themselves are fed from the mains, to give the correct pressure.

During the time that Richmond Park was a hunting-ground and little else, its springs acted as drinking places for the deer and other game. A map made for Charles I at the time of the park's enclosure shows no standing water, though there are two central streams in addition to what is identifiable as the Beverley Brook, the small river which flows through

135

the east corner of the park from near Robin Hood Gate to a point north-west of Roehampton Gate. In fact, the two Pen Ponds, as well as the other smaller ones scattered around the park, are man-made. The latter are for the most part old gravel pits, these having been a natural source of revenue. These small ponds, together with whatever springs remained after extensive drainage of the land, continue to be frequented by the deer.

The two larger ponds have a different history. A small tributary of the Beverley Brook, whose course may be traced from near Ham Cross Plantation, is known to have been dammed about 1636 and at a later date accounted for the construction of the Upper and Lower Pen Ponds. Yet these do not appear on Charles I's map. But two lakes of roughly the same dimensions as at present, and separated by a path, are shown on John Rocque's Survey of London, 1741–5. This is proof that they cannot have been made at the instigation of Princess Amelia, the youngest daughter of George II, as is popularly supposed. However, though the Pen Ponds must have antedated the princess's rangership, it is thought that she altered their shape, though this could have been caused by natural silting. Almost certainly she gave them their present name, which is believed to be derived from nearby deer pens. In the nineteenth century, however, they were temporarily known as the Canals. In any event John Rocque's map, as well as one made by John Eyre for George II in the fourth year of Princess Amelia's rangership, shows streams leading from springs some distance to the south-west and north-west, and feeding the Upper Pen Pond. The shape of the ponds has not altered much since the mid-eighteenth century. They cover more than twenty-four acres at two levels, and are separated by a causeway in the centre of which there is a sluice. The Beverley Brook takes the overflow.

In recent times mains water, which already supplied the residential properties, was used to maintain the level of various reservoirs in the park. Otherwise water for general use has been pumped from the Thames to a reservoir not far from Pembroke Lodge, from which Kew Gardens was supplied by gravity. At the time of writing, plans are materialising for the total replacement of the old system by mains water. Pardonable anxiety may be felt for the rhododendrons, azaleas, heaths and other lime-detesting plants and shrubs of the Isabella Woodland

Garden, which cannot be expected to tolerate the hardness of Thames water, nor perhaps the degree of chlorination which has come to be accepted as a feature of modern human existence.

The fact that Greenwich Park relies upon supplies piped in by the Metropolitan Water Board from near the Blackheath boundary to a circular reservoir near the east end of Great Cross Avenue is an entirely different matter. Though unromantic, this is a practical necessity. Greenwich is a small park, and on two levels. Besides, its soil consists of gravel and sand, so that far from releasing natural water it absorbs it rapidly. Two days after a thorough soaking the flowerbeds can be parched. The lake in the Flower Garden and the Children's Boating Pool are the only two pieces of standing water.

These are the facts of the parks' water supply, but there is still speculation about a strange pattern of brick-lined passages running beneath Greenwich Park, but which almost certainly had some connection with Greenwich Palace, now destroyed. Various theories have been advanced following a nineteenth-century survey and a more extensive exploration about eight years ago. The general layout is of a series of tunnels, some of which may have originated as lime-working passages, or which could have been intended as escape routes from the Tudor palace. However the theory that they are water conduits is borne out by their being brick-lined and brick-based, but sloping to a central lead-lined gully. Most of the passages are about two feet six inches wide, and nearly six feet high at the centre of the vaulting. The main arm runs south from the Conduit House on Conduit Avenue near King George Street Gate, then branches right towards Vanbrugh Fields and on to a point near One Tree Hill, near the centre of the park. Another passage is known to exist under Crooms Hill, Hyde Vale, West Grove Lane and Point Hill, all outside the park. It is also believed that a further tunnel ran south from the Greenwich Park system to Blackheath. Unfortunately, all this is academic. The tunnels are subject to collapse, and in fact have from time to time betrayed their existence by subsidence. As a precaution all known entrances have now been sealed. The best source of information on the various surveys—both ancient and immediately before final closure—is the Greenwich Local History Library, Mycenae Road, SE3.

I

16

BIRDS AND BEASTS

The fauna of the Royal Parks fall into two categories: the native bird and animal populations which have adapted themselves to changes in their natural habitats, not only by reason of an instinct for survival, but also due to an enlightened parks policy which provides sanctuaries for such important operations as breeding in an otherwise densely human-infested environment; and those protected creatures, such as deer and ornamental wildfowl, which require a degree of management, including feeding and numerical control. It is also in the tradition of the Royal Parks that they operate nothing in the style of a menagerie, like the one which existed for James I's pleasure in St James's Park. There are no cages and no enclosures except in Greenwich Park, where fallow deer are fenced in for their own wellbeing. The Royal Zoological Gardens, territorially part of Regent's Park, are a major exception.

The birds of the Royal Parks, both wild and ornamental, are the concern of a dedicated body of men who protect, watch, observe, count and generally put themselves at the service of this most attractive branch of wildlife. Each park has one or more bird sanctuaries, to which no ordinary member of the public has access, and the existence of which ensures the survival of a great many species in the heart of the metropolis.

A select committee was appointed in 1947, the terms of reference being 'to advise the Minister of Works [now the Secretary of State for the Environment] on Bird Sanctuaries in the Royal Parks and in other open spaces in his control in England and Wales'. Reports were issued every two years, and published by the Stationery Office. These were primarily based upon the records of official but unpaid observers attached to specific parks or areas. This meant that the reports tended to

138

be uneven, according to the amount of time which it was possible to devote to a self-imposed and sometimes strenuous task. Though the constitution of the select committee and its methods are excellent, within certain unavoidable limitations, public information is now to be issued in the form of an annual pamphlet. The one covering 1971 and 1972 will be available, free, at sales points in the Royal Parks and elsewhere. A copy is also to be included in Eric Simms's paperback *Wild Life in the Royal Parks*, which will be obtainable from HMSO bookshop in High Holborn, or by mail order. The new pamphlet will not be available before this present book goes to press, but it is understood to contain some significant changes, mainly aimed at simplification. It will include the chairman's report, notes on important developments, and a table of observations gleaned from the voluntary observers appointed by the Department of the Environment, usually after nomination by the London Natural History Society. Although teams of two or three men have in this way been allocated to most of the Royal Parks, during the period immediately under review no observers have been forthcoming for Regent's Park and Primrose Hill, nor for Greenwich Park which, however, is covered by the London Natural History Society. The observers serve three years at a stretch, and are reappointed for similar terms as long as their health, endurance and other interests permit.

A table of birds recorded as having been sighted in the Royal Parks is given in the HMSO reports, including counts of birds in Kew Gardens and Osterley. These are classified in species according to the Wetmore Order, and indications are given as to those which are known to have bred, possibly did breed, or have simply been sighted. St James's Park, Green Park, Hampton Court and Bushy Park show increases in species of birds over preceding years, while Richmond Park's total has declined from 100 to 93 species, a figure which includes 4 fewer breeding species of birds. As demonstration of the dedication of the official observers, and also of the importance of their work, it may be mentioned here that in the 1969–70 report almost a hundred different species of birds were identified in Hyde Park and Kensington Gardens. A proportion of these were seasonal visitors, and what the report classes as vagrants, but it was estimated that from one-third to one-half of the total of species in each park actually nested there. In 1972 observers identified breeding pairs of the great crested grebe in both Hyde Park and Regent's Park, a development which excited ornithologists.

Regent's Park provides varied habitats in the form of shrubberies, gardens, trees and water, while the open grassland used for recreational purposes attracts birds of passage. In fact, some migrants such as the blackcap, whitethroat and willow warbler are showing a tendency to remain in the park to nest. Common birds, such as wrens, various tits, dunnocks and finches are on the increase, while woodpeckers and stock doves are on the decline. Rarities, as far as London is concerned, such as the great grey shrike, hawfinch, little owl and crossbill have been observed. Swifts and house martins come to the park for the insects on which they feed, and which are to be found in swarms over the lake. As in so many other places, butterflies in Regent's Park are becoming fewer, though red underwing moths still haunt the trees, and red admirals, tortoiseshells and cabbage white butterflies continue to be attracted by the flowers. Bees, thought to be commuters from Hampstead, play their part in the cycle of nature by pollinating the park's flowering cherries.

One of Regent's Park's chief ornithological prides is its heronry, situated on an island in the lake, and protected by a boom from marauders by boat, yet still requiring extreme vigilance. This breeding colony in Inner London is something of an achievement, especially in view of the fact that Richmond Park has lost its own complement. In 1972 there were seven nests in evidence in Regent's Park, though there was some uncertainty as to the number of mated birds these represented. The parent birds, finding the lake's fish inadequate, and having demolished Bedford College's supply of goldfish, now fly to reservoirs near Hounslow for supplies. Regent's Park is one of the only two Royal Parks—the other being St James's Park—to need a birdkeeper for pinioned waterfowl. The former holder of the office having retired, a younger man is being trained to undertake the care of the lake's population. Primrose Hill, although so close to Regent's Park is, because of its height and comparative treelessness, chiefly remarkable as a vantage point from which to observe migrants on the wing.

140

Interesting birds seen in Hyde Park and Kensington Gardens during recent years include, as well as the great crested grebe already mentioned, Slavonian grebes, dunlins, black redstarts and hawfinches. Bullfinches, elsewhere a pest because of their incorrigible destructiveness to fruit blossom, are proudly claimed to have nested in these parks. Hard winters bring in a greater variety of birds than usual. In 1970 a pair of mute swans flew in and nested near the end of the Long Water in Kensington Gardens, where they succeeded in rearing a family of six in full view of London's perambulators.

Songbirds have become particularly attached to St James's Park, and the lake attracts various wildfowl, who live in harmony with the introduced species. Mallards, as usual, breed without circumspection, though mainly on the islands, and also some tufted ducks. Moorhens, coots and the European pochard are in permanent residence. Recorded rarities include a grasshopper warbler (heard but not seen), willow warblers and chiffchaffs, and one solitary kingfisher, as well as a wintering red-headed smew (the female only is red-headed). Carrion crows are the bane of existence for St James's Park's full-time birdkeeper, Mr Arthur May.

Twenty-four examples of pinioned waterfowl are illustrated on noticeboards at the edge of St James's Park lake. Here the marginal paths do not exactly follow the edge of the water; shrubberies are frequently interposed, or, alternatively, a narrow low-railed strip of lawn. However, the real heart of birdlife is Duck Island, a sanctuary vital to the existence of the waterfowl. The public is excluded, the most obvious reason being that otherwise the island would be no sanctuary. Here are located the offices of the birdkeeper; his delightful but rather ramshackle dispensary to which London citizens, halting at what amounts to a drawbridge, are apt to bring sick or distressed birds; yards where 'pensioners' get underfoot; pens for the sick, motherless or strayed; incubators; bays for catching birds in need of attention; privet hedges so spattered with starling excrement that they have to be washed periodically—all adding up to a hidden world of wildfowl lore shared, not at all discordantly, with the modern impressive pumping station.

Mr May is another Dr Dolittle, not only talking to but living with and for his birds. He mourns individuals, such as the pelicans, which 'pass over'. It is difficult to make people understand that these comic and lovable birds should not be fed; their chance of survival is increased if they are limited to their normal scheduled meal at 4 pm. The hatchery on Duck Island is his special concern. It requires twenty-four-hour attention, not only when the eggs are in the incubators, but for several weeks afterwards, until the young birds have reached a safe, feathered stage of development. Pochards in particular are a worry. Because their legs are set far back, they are weak walkers and when they fall they have difficulty in righting themselves without assistance. He has also had to train himself to be philosophical about such things as Carolina ducks, who can be perverse enough to nest on ledges in nearby Victoria Street, above the traffic, with the result that their babies plummet to the ground.

Greenwich Park is on a regular flight path, and many migrants have been observed in transit, or when they have dropped in for a rest, a favoured spot being a damp patch east of General Wolfe's statue. Snipe and woodcock have been observed in the Deer Park. As for the regular population of this park, woodpigeons and stock doves abound, and there have also been sightings of collared doves and turtle doves. Of the smaller birds, the lesser spotted woodpecker has so far been unsuccessful in nesting, and was not sighted in 1972. But the park's wrens are increasing in numbers since the disastrous hard winter of 1962–3, when they were all but wiped out. To sum up, the number of species in decline following neighbourhood development which isolated what is a comparatively small park, has started to show an upward movement following improvements to the Wilderness Bird Sanctuary.

Bushy Park, with its farmland characteristics, has the greatest number of breeding species—about forty-nine in 1969 and 1970. Pheasants and partridges are among these. The most interesting of breeding pairs include little grebes, stock doves, goldcrests, lesser whitethroats and chiffchaffs. Other not very common birds to be observed in Bushy and Hampton Court Home parks include the goldeneye, goosander, curlew, sedge warbler, pied flycatcher and lesser warbler. Hampton Court Gardens attract many of the commoner garden birds,

142

many of whom nest oblivious of daytime crowds. House martins favour the crannies and eaves of the palace, though their home-building proclivities are not encouraged by those people responsible for the fabric of this lovely building. In Bushy and Hampton Court parks, as in Richmond, the waterfowl are the responsibility of the gamekeeper.

Richmond's Pen Ponds attract numerous aquatic birds, including different types of gull. In keeping with the spirit of this naturalistic park, the Committee on Bird Sanctuaries recommended that no ornamental, tame or pinioned waterfowl should be introduced. The result is that wild birds do not have to face competition from a pampered opposition, and migrants appreciate the free space. The park's plantations make heaven-sent territories for a wide range of woodland birds. Rarities have included a red-necked grebe, kestrels, and one Montagu harrier as a fleeting visitor. In line with the park's history, there are snipe and woodcock, pheasants and partridges, some of which are hand-reared, though never shot. During George II's reign no less than 3,000 wild turkeys were preserved in the park after the manner of pheasants. They roosted in the ivied outer walls and pollarded oaks. Then, in the words of an authority writing about a century later 'early in the reign of George III that benevolent monarch ordered the extirpation of the tempting exotic Gallinacea'. Their crime was that they had proved irresistible to poachers. Cuckoos and owls (barn, tawny, little and even the rare short-eared owl) make their contribution to Richmond, and larks abound. There are also jackdaws, birds which have virtually disappeared from Inner London, a fact difficult to explain because they are so readily domesticated. Carrion crows are a menace here as elsewhere, and magpies have been blamed for causing fires by picking up smouldering cigarette ends thrown out of cars, then dropping them hastily in the trees.

The Upper Pen Pond is sheltered by a crescent of woodland. Once it was a game preserve and now, since there is no game in a sporting sense, it is a bird sanctuary, and one stretch of water has been railed off for the benefit of waterfowl. It and the other ponds are on open ground, so much so that in the last war they had to be drained, to prevent their being an obvious landmark for enemy aircraft. Before being refilled they were cleaned, and then restocked with coarse fish taken from the

143

reservoirs of the Metropolitan Water Board. From time to time in the past, artificial islands of 'rafts' were created in both Pen Ponds for the encouragement of nesting waterfowl, the method being to build a palisade of willow stakes into which sods of turf and rushes could be packed. These willows (or sallies) tended to take root and stabilise the enclosure. This hit or miss technique often produced irregular 'natural' shapes. Later, when the head of the Upper Pen Pond was railed off, Norfolk reeds were introduced from the Broads. These established themselves after being augmented in 1934 by stock brought from Windsor Great Park.

Though birds are a delight to everyone, as well as having their knowledgeable following, the deer of London's Royal Parks may have greater, because more obvious, appeal. They constitute one of the chief attractions of Richmond, Bushy and Hampton Court parks as well as being an incidental feature of Greenwich. The deer are authoritatively considered to be the direct descendants of ones which roamed free in the royal hunting grounds during Henry VIII's reign. In every case their numbers have to be controlled in proportion to the space, grazing and fodder available. Where vegetation is unfenced, the purpose is to provide cover for the animals; the trees then assume mushroom shapes, their leaves and branches being eaten off to the level to which a rearing fullgrown stag can reach.

The Royal Parks' deer consist of red and fallow deer, the former being distinguished by their greater size and the latter by their slender shapes and dappled pelts. The red deer are kept in the larger parks: about 100 in Bushy and over 200 in Richmond. Bushy Park has about 220 fallow deer, Hampton Court Home Park (where they act as an additional hazard to golfers) 126, Richmond Park 395 and Greenwich a mere 25 in 1972. The two breeds of deer remain in separate groups, and certainly do not interbreed; in fact, their rutting seasons differ by a month. The antique nomenclature of deer is fascinating: females of the red deer, especially during and after their third year, are hinds, while female fallow deer are known as does. The adult male of the fallow deer is termed a buck, whereas the equivalent male red deer is a stag. A buck in his second year, one recognisable by his straight unbranched horns, is a pricket, while a female of the same age has no name of her own, and is known as a pricket's sister. And, while the young of red deer are rather plebeianly called calves, the Bambi-like fallow deer youngsters are fawns. It is quite usual for a single hind to assume responsibility for a 'crêche' of young while their own mothers are otherwise occupied.

Deer range freely in Bushy, Hampton Court and Richmond parks, except where crops, plantations or gardens are at risk. Outer main gates, through which there is a constant flow of traffic, are always manned. Pedestrian gates are constructed on the barrel or kissing-gate system, and therefore secure. The Deer Park in Greenwich is a well-wooded triangle, the outer park wall forming two of its sides. On the third there are vantage points provided with seats, where the public can look into small spaces and rides cut into this private world. The twenty-five fallow deer (eleven mating couples) are tamer than the free-ranging deer of the bigger parks, and consequently need more attention. When necessary, veterinary advice is forthcoming from the Equine Research Establishment at Newmarket which, strangely, has a special Deer Research branch. Deer are prone to brucellosis, a disease usually associated with cattle, against which measures aimed at nationwide eradication are in operation. Most uncharacteristically, Richmond's fallow deer were decimated by rabies in 1886–7. Though the disease is not endemic to the species, it is thought that they contracted it from rabid stray dogs. To prevent disease in the limited ground available for the Greenwich deer, a third of the Deer Park there is ploughed every year, herbal strips are sown and mineral licks provided.

Captive deer have to be fed from November to March, since their environment even in the larger parks is not altogether natural. Crops are grown in Bushy Park for this express purpose: oats, beans, roots and maize. The latter crop so far has been ensiled, but experiments are being made with a new variety which could mature regularly in our erratic climate. Locust beans from carob trees are imported from Cyprus, and fed in the form of meal. Bushy and Hampton Court parks are almost self-supporting, but Richmond Park, on the other hand, buys in its fodder with the exception of hay. Traditionally feeding was done in pens, but nowadays fair distribution is ensured by spreading the fodder under trees.

145

Without mincing matters, it must be admitted that annual culling forms an important part of the management of parkland deer. Elimination of the aged and weaklings from a herd by humane methods forms an acceptable substitute for hunting. Otherwise, use is made of dart projectors, similar to guns, which fire an anaesthetic immobilising agent. These firearms are imported under licence from the United States, as they are not permitted to be manufactured in this country. They have almost entirely replaced the crossbow formerly used for firing the darts. The superintendents, being servants of the Crown, are exempt from gun-licensing regulations.

Females are culled from mid-November to mid-January, and males during August and September. The object is to keep herd numbers down to manageable proportions, and though an allocation of venison by royal warrant is a highly esteemed privilege, no attempt is made to slaughter animals for the express purpose of continuing a custom said to date from the twelfth century. Whereas in 1773, 273 bucks were shared out, the 1972 list contained an allocation of ninety-eight quarters. Entitlement to venison is based partly upon early charters. Allocations were also made to landowners who had surrendered land for incorporation into royal demesnes. Nowadays the venison goes mainly to occupants of major ministerial posts, and to holders of office who have some connection with the parks and their deer. A random sample of major recipients includes the Grand Falconer of England, the Archbishops of York and Canterbury, the Prime Minister and the Lord Chief Justice, while a second list includes the Mayor of Kingston-upon-Thames, the Captain of the Queen's Bodyguard of the Yeomen of the Guard and the Sheriff and Officers of the City of London. Understandably the first list is headed by four quarters 'for the Service of the Royal Table'. The meat is for the personal use of recipients, and the allocation is approved by Royal Sign Manual, the phrasing of which is in resounding terms:

THESE ARE TO AUTHORISE AND REQUIRE YOU to sign AND ISSUE the proper WARRANTS to THE RANGERS and KEEPERS OF OUR FORESTS AND PARKS to deliver for the service of OUR OWN TABLE and for THE LORDS and

OTHERS mentioned in the accompanying LIST NO I accustomed to OUR ROYAL FAVOUR one QUARTER or more of a DOE of this SEASON according to the number placed against their respective names: AND FURTHER TO AUTHORISE and REQUIRE YOU in similar WARRANTS to THE RANGERS AND KEEPERS OF OUR FORESTS AND PARKS to deliver for the LORDS AND OTHERS mentioned in the accompanying list No II one QUARTER or more of a DOE according to the number placed against their respective names.

This royal venison warrant is signed by the sovereign and issued to the Department of the Environment, after which it goes to the park superintendents concerned. Any surplus remaining after the requirements of the royal warrant have been met is sold in Smithfield Market at a nominal charge intended to cover distribution costs only.

Regular and selective culling should not offend even the most squeamish persons. The operation is necessary as a substitute for the natural law of the survival of the fittest. The public should take pleasure in the evidence of their eyes: the perfect specimens to be seen in these four Royal Parks. In Richmond, the first sight of the deer frequently consists of horns apparently sprouting from bracken, in weird shapes reminiscent of Sidney Nolan's paintings of dead Australian trees. The parkland deer should be approached with caution—never with dogs—and certainly not fed. The months when extreme care must be exercised are October, the beginning of the rutting season, and from May to July, when the animals are on the defensive following giving birth and weathering the critical first weeks of rearing the young.

Foxes can be a menace to both fawns and calves. They will in fact take the newly-dropped young, a specially hazardous time being the first twenty-four hours of life, when mothers will have concealed their young in bracken or other undergrowth, and left them unguarded. Conservationists are pleased to know that despite their classification as vermin foxes have not been eradicated from the Royal Parks. Bushy and Hampton Court parks contain fewer earths than previously and an occasional wanderer penetrates into Greenwich. It is a reflection upon modern times that these courageous, sporting and romantic animals appear to have become degenerate. Nowadays they seem to prefer scavenging in the dustbins of suburban Wimbledon, Hampton and the like rather than stalking their traditional prey in open spaces.

Although for some years neither fox earths nor fox cubs have been observed in Richmond Park, there are still some badger sets there. Though controversy exists, these attractive and nocturnal animals are only minimally destructive though they have been known to flatten crops by rolling in them. They are subjected to no official interference in the Royal Parks. Beavers, after which the Beverley Brook which cuts across the eastern corner of Richmond Park is named, have been unknown in England since the eleventh or twelfth centuries.

Though hare populations escaped the disease, myxomatosis took its toll of rabbits in all the parks. But they are now returning, in some cases having learned to live above ground rather than in infected burrows. Yet the superintendent in charge of Hampton Court and Bushy parks estimates that even now, from every ten sighted, one rabbit at least bears symptoms of the disease. But even healthy rabbits have to be culled. They are usually dealt with before many park users are abroad. In Regent's Park, where they infested the Bird Sanctuary, they could not be shot for fear of disturbing the legitimate inhabitants, and ferrets and nets were used; the result fell far short of a clean sweep, and as such must satisfy those who, while approving control of vermin, do not favour annihilation. Rabbits are returning, too, to the Dell in Hyde Park, that small fenced area at the foot of the Serpentine and close to the roar of Knightsbridge traffic. Their reappearance is artificial, and by human agency, in that members of the public have been known to use this enclosure as a conscience-saving disposal unit for unwanted pets. The resulting hybrids come in a variety of colours, helped along by the notorious promiscuity of the species.

Grey squirrels, in spite of being so charming in the eyes of the beholder, are a nuisance to everyone responsible for gardens. They are to be found in all the parks, and are very tame. But they are death, literally, to many bedding plants such as polyanthus, because they relish the centres as delicacies, as well as doing untold damage to newly planted bulbs, tulips being their favourites. Since these little animals breed twice yearly, the authorities have to close their eyes to their engaging cuddliness in an attempt to keep numbers within bounds. It is understood that experiments are afoot elsewhere to feed contraceptives disguised as nuts to grey squirrels. Royal Parks' policy with regard to this practice has not yet been announced.

Hedgehogs, universally approved, occur in greatest number in Hampton Court and Bushy parks. Up till a fairly recent date otters visited Greenwich Park, but for some years none have been sighted.

Within the context of the wildlife of the parks, it is encouraging that in 1972 a Nature Trail for primary schoolchildren was organised under the auspices of the Friends of Richmond Park. The operation was conducted under close supervision to prevent environmental disturbance, and on-the-spot briefing was adopted as an alternative to notices and signposts. At first there were doubts as to the project's survival, the snag being regulations which forbid coaches from travelling through, parking in, or even setting down passengers in the park; yet distances from any one gate put most of the most interesting, remote and natural parts well out of reach for young pedestrians. But now, happily, the regulations have been bent for this one exception, and a new trail for secondary schools is a possibility.

BIBLIOGRAPHY

Ashton, John. *Hyde Park from Domesday to Date* (1896)

Barton, N. L. *The Lost Rivers of London* (1962)

Boulton, W. B. *The Amusements of London*, Vol 2 (1841)

Braybrooke, Neville. *London Green, the Story of Kensington Gardens, Hyde Park, Green Park and St James's Park* (1959)

Brown, Thomas. *Amusements Serious and Comical, Calculated for the Meridian of London* (1700), ed A. L. Hayward (1927)

Butler, E. M. (ed). *A Regency Visitor: The Letters of Prince Puckler-Muskau* (1957)

Cecil, The Hon Mrs E. *London Parks and Gardens* (1907)

Chadwick, George F. *The Park and the Town* (1966)

Church, Richard. *The Royal Parks of London* (HMSO, 1956)

Cole, Nathan. 'The Royal Parks and Gardens of London, Their History and Mode of Embellishment', *Journal of Horticultural Office* (1877)

Dancy, Eric. *Hyde Park* (1937)

Davis, H. L. *Memorials of the Hamlet of Knightsbridge* (1859)

Davis, Terence. *John Nash, the Prince Regent's Architect* (1966)

Dunbar, Janet. *A Prospect of Richmond* (1966)

Elmes, James. *Metropolitan Improvements* (1827)

Fletcher Jones, Pamela. *Richmond Park, Portrait of a Royal Playground* (1972)

Foord, A. S. *Springs, Streams and Spas of London* (1910)

Fox, Helen. *André le Nôtre, Garden Architect to Kings* (1963)

Garside, Bernard. *The Manor, Lordship and Great Parks of Hampton Court during the Sixteenth and Seventeenth Centuries* (1951)

Gibbs-Smith, C. H. *The Great Exhibition of 1851* (HMSO, 1950)

Gleichen, Lord Edward. *London's Open-Air Statuary* (1928)

Hall, H. R. H. *Round the Year in Richmond Park* (1923)

Hamilton, Olive and Nigel. *Royal Greenwich* (Greenwich Bookshop, 1969)

Harrison, Michael. *London Beneath the Pavement* (1961)

Hawksmoor, Nicholas. *History of Greenwich Hospital* (1727)

——. *Remarks on the Founding and Carrying On of the Buildings at Greenwich, for the Perusal of Parliament* (1728)

Hudson, W. H. *A Hind in Richmond Park* (1922)

——. *Birds in London* (London 1898; reprinted Newton Abbot 1969)

Hyams, Edward. *Capability Brown and Humphrey Repton* (1971)

Jellicoe, G. A. *Studies in Landscape Design*, Vol 3 (1960)

Larwood, Jacob. *The Story of the London Parks* (c 1825)

Law, Ernest. *The History of Hampton Court Palace*, Vols 1–3 (1885–91)

Minney, Rubeigh H. *Hampton Court* (1972)

Norden, John. *Notes on London and Westminster* (1592)

Ormsby, H. *London on the Thames* (2nd edition, 1928)

Samuel, E. C. *The Villas in Regent's Park and Their Residents* (1959)

Sands, M. *The Gardens of Hampton Court* (1950)

Saunders, Ann. *Regent's Park, a Study of the Development of the Area from 1086 to the Present Day* (Newton Abbot, 1969)

Simms, Eric. *Wild Life in the Royal Parks* (in preparation HMSO, 1974)

Stow, John. *Survey of London* (1598)

——. *Survey of London* 'corrected, improved and very much enlarged by John Strype' (1720)

——. *The Annales of England* (1605)

Summerson, Sir John. *John Nash, Architect to King George IV* (1962)

Timbs, J. *The Year Book of Facts* (1851)

Turberville, G. *The Noble Art of Venerie or Hunting* (1575)

Tweedie, Mrs A. *Hyde Park, Its History and Romance* (1908)

Walford, Edward. *Old and New London* (1873)

Ward, Cyril. *Royal Gardens* (1912)

Webster, A. D. *The Regent's Park and Primrose Hill: History and Antiquities* (1911)

——. *Greenwich Park: Its History and Associations* (1902, reprinted 1971)

BIBLIOGRAPHY

Whitaker, Ben and Brown, Kenneth. *Parks for People* (1971)
Yates, Edward. *Hampton Court* (1935)

OFFICIAL PUBLICATIONS

Bird Life in the Royal Parks 1969–70 (HMSO, 1971)
Future of Regent's Park Terraces, Third Statement by the Crown Estate Commissioners (HMSO, 1962)
Greater London Development Scheme—Statement (GLC, 1969)
Reports of the Advisory Committee on Forestry (HMSO, 1954–64)
Surveys of the Use of Open Spaces, Vol I (GLC, 1968)

ACKNOWLEDGEMENTS

I wish to thank the Department of the Environment, particularly in the persons of Mike Davey and Ian Saberton, and Mr Hare, the Bailiff of the Royal Parks, for placing themselves and their knowledge at my disposal while I was gathering information for this book. The individual superintendents of the Royal Parks and their staff at every level, and Inspector Warren of the Metropolitan Police, all did everything in their power to assist my explorations, and there are many other knowledgeable and dedicated people who gave me their time and the benefit of their experience. Though these are too many to name, I hope they will accept this overall expression of gratitude.

K

INDEX